Soul
AGREEMENTS

Other New Age Books by Dick Sutphen

Simon & Schuster Pocket Books
You Were Born Again to Be Together
Past Lives, Future Loves
Unseen Influences
Predestined Love
Finding Your Answers Within
Earthly Purpose
The Oracle Within

Valley of the Sun Publishing
Master of Life Manual
Enlightenment Transcripts
Lighting the Light Within
Past-Life Therapy in Action
Sedona: Psychic Energy Vortexes
Heart Magic
The Spiritual Path Guidebook
Reinventing Yourself
Radical Spirituality
Simple Solutions
New Age Short Stories
With Your Spirit Guide's Help

Nightingale Conant (Book and Audio)
Mind Travel
Hypnology
Self Mastery

By Tara Sutphen

Valley of the Sun Publishing
Blame It on Your Past Lives

Audio CDs and Videos
Dick and Tara have over 300 self-help, self-exploration, and meditation programs available:

www.dicksutphen.com

Soul Agreements

DICK SUTPHEN
with TARA SUTPHEN

HAMPTON ROADS
PUBLISHING COMPANY, INC.

Cover design by Marjoram Productions
Cover digital imagery © 2004 PictureQuest/IT Stock Free

Excerpts from *The Initiation* by Donald Schnell
used by permission of Inner Ocean Publishing.

Hampton Roads Publishing Company, Inc.
1125 Stoney Ridge Road
Charlottesville, VA 22902

434-296-2772
fax: 434-296-5096
e-mail: hrpc@hrpub.com
www.hrpub.com

If you are unable to order this book from your local
bookseller, you may order directly from the publisher.
Call 1-800-766-8009, toll-free.

Library of Congress Cataloging-in-Publication Data

Sutphen, Richard.
    Soul agreements / Dick Sutphen, with Tara Sutphen.
        p. cm.
    Summary: "Examines the impact reincarnation and karma can have on
individuals. Gives specific cases as well as more general information and
shows that it is possible to make the most of one's destiny and overcome
negativity to create success and love"—Provided by publisher.
    Includes bibliographical references.
    ISBN 1-57174-442-8 (5-1/2x8-1/2 tp : alk. paper)
    1. Reincarnation. 2. Karma--Miscellanea. I. Sutphen, Tara. II. Title.
BL515.S88 2005
133.9'01'35--dc22
                                                2004030488

ISBN 10: 1-57174-442-8
ISBN 13: 978-1-57174-442-5
10 9 8 7 6 5 4 3 2
Printed on acid-free, recycled paper in Canada

Acknowledgments

Dick Sutphen: I want to acknowledge and thank my wife, Tara, especially for her psychic and astrological work on this book. Thanks to my agent, Bob Silverstein, and to Frank DeMarco, chairman of Hampton Roads Publishing. Who would have thought our talk at the Universal Light Expo in Columbus, Ohio, would end up manifesting *Soul Agreements*. Special thanks to my friend Gloria Jewell, who inspired me to move this book from an idea to a reality by volunteering her sister Geri as a phenomenal case history. Also to Lisa Rojany Buccieri, my L.A. editor, who always keeps me on the proper grammatical and conceptual paths. Thanks to my personal astrologer, Lee Holloway, for her valuable guidance, and to the people whose case histories are shared here. Several are friends: Shauna, Meghan, Richard, Diana, and Patti. Others became friends after we worked together. I also want to acknowledge all of our children, friends, and relatives whom Tara has listed below.

Tara Sutphen: Many thanks and blessings to the treasured people in my life who helped me develop my metaphysical abilities. My husband, Richard. My children: William, Hunter, and Cheyenne. My stepchildren: Scott, Todd, Steve, Jessi, and Travis. Also Sage Dakota. And the children's beloveds: Duane Fletcher, Carie Hoover, and Kimberly Bedgio.

My mother, Marianne Corey; my siblings: Timothy Marshall, Scott, Jason, and Sumire McKean, and Amy and Marc Beaver. My nieces: Brionna, Shannon, and Audrey. My nephews: Aaron and Phillip. My friends: Marie Lehman, Marla Maples, Shane Stanley, Shauna Blais, Katherine Brooks, Patrick Smith, Richard Christian Matheson, Diana Mullen, Kathy Watson, Mary Casey, Aline Ball, Robi Banks, Mary Blakslee, Pam Litz, Peggy Fields, Tonya McArthur, Terry Wallace, Dianette Strange, Don Tinling, Tiffany Silver, Lindi Holland, and Kara Soufer. To my teachers and healers: Barbara May, Helene Kayal, Patti Conklin, Fatima and Rhandy, and Dr. Terry Dulin. To my clan: McKeans of California, Risches of Alaska, the Blackfoot and Cherokee Nations, and the Pagans of Scotland. And to my guide Abenda, who is as real as the people on Earth. She is an angel dedicated to help mankind by offering wisdom and comfort. I feel fortunate to know her, to work with her, to love her. "The key to enlightenment is compassion," is her primary message.

Contents

Preface

August 1989, upstate New York: Mark, 24, drove the company pickup down a steep three-mile hill on his way to work as a heavy-equipment operator. Jeff, a friend and company mechanic, was sipping coffee in the passenger seat. Jeff was tired and had asked Mark to drive. The two men talked about their lives, their wives, and the joy Jeff was experiencing with his baby daughter.

At the bottom of the hill, construction crews had narrowed the country road to a single lane. Mark stopped, the last of ten cars awaiting traffic clearance. Glancing into the rearview mirror, he noticed the Pepsi truck speeding down the hill only seconds before it careened into the back of his pickup truck at 60 miles an hour.

The gas tank exploded in a hailstorm of tortured metal—a fireball engulfing both trucks.

Jeff died on impact. Mark was thrown through the small back window of the vehicle into a raging bed of fire.

Although burned over forty percent of his body, Mark survived.

An investigation revealed that someone had cut the brake lines on the Pepsi truck, which had been driven by a scab driver during a strike.

Shortly after the accident, Mark's wife divorced her disfigured and wheelchair-bound husband.

Today, fifteen years later, Mark is still confined to a wheelchair and has experienced sixty reconstructive operations. His spinal cord continues to degenerate, providing a major life challenge.

According to Mark's astrology, on the day of the accident, a dozen planetary aspects were focused upon violence, debt, malevolence, destructiveness, and catastrophe. Behind the scenes, retribution and retaliation were indicated. Other aspects of his birth chart indicated soul-goal cleanup, divorce, and self-undoing.

In other words, an accident was fated to occur at this time. Mark was born to have the experience.

Introduction

After 30 years of researching reincarnation and karma, I have come to some conclusions about destiny and the degree to which our earthly path is mapped out. Prior to our birth, while still in spirit, we each decide upon the karma we will confront during our life. In Mark's case, described in the preface, he decided to reincarnate to experience major suffering—the kind of suffering he may have perpetrated upon others in a past life.

Your karmic road map is your astrology chart. Given the date, time, and place of your birth, a talented astrologer can read your life, and by progressing the chart into the present, advise you about the planetary cycles currently affecting you both positively and negatively. Each of us plans our life to experience different degrees of destiny and free will. One person will structure his life plan to include predestined opportunities and to allow very little free will, while another person plans her incarnation to include minimal predestined events and considerable free will. How an incarnation is structured has a lot to do with the kinds of lessons needing to be learned.

In three of my previous books, *You Were Born Again to Be Together, Earthly Purpose,* and *Predestined Love* (Simon & Schuster Pocket

Books), I explored the concept of destiny through romantic relationships. In this volume, my investigations expand to include a variety of cases: a woman born with a severe disability, a couple who came together to experience tragedy, and others who incarnated to be famous, or influential, or to become healers.

I am convinced that even for those who minimize the plausibility of predestined events, major relationships are fated. In other words, we all reincarnated to be together with our parents, lovers, mates, children, and others who affect our lives in the most meaningful ways.

Think of your life as a story you wrote while in spirit, prior to incarnating upon the Earth. This may not be the way you want it to be, but it is what is. I would prefer total free will—to create my own reality—to mold my destiny in response to my desires on a day-to-day basis. But from a higher perspective, since we chose our path prior to birth, we do have absolute freedom. We chose the pain and problems, the pleasure and joy, but we do not consciously remember the decisions we made in spirit. And no matter what we experience, we always have the free will to respond with love or with fear. Karmically, the experience is a test and not important in itself, while our responses determine if we have learned our lesson.

The more self-actualized we are, the less likely we will be adversely affected by negative life experiences. We incarnated to rise above our fear-based emotions and to learn to experience life with unconditional acceptance—without expectations, judgment, blame, or need to control others. In Zen, this is called "detached mind"— the ability to enjoy all the pleasures life has to offer, but when outside conditions change, allowing the negativity to flow through you without affecting you. In other words, if through awareness and by altering your viewpoint you're no longer affected by a problem, you don't have a problem—even though nothing about the problem situation may have changed.

1

A Changed New York Skyline

"Our hour is marked, and no one can claim a moment of life beyond what fate has predestined."
—Napoleon Bonaparte

Explorations of destiny are often part of the seminars and workshops Tara and I conduct around the world. "A changed New York skyline" was the primary millennium vision perceived by the participants in the "New Day Seminar"—conducted in six California cities in 1997 and a five-day seminar in Missoula, Montana, April 1998. One hundred forty attendees at the Los Angeles Whole Life Expo workshop, November 1997, also reported their visions, in addition to those who participated in the January 1998 "Millennium Projection Research Project." (For a nominal fee, readers of our newsletter were sent a Hypnotic Progression tape, which instructed them to psychically perceive the future.)

I believe we view the future clairvoyantly by stepping outside of time and space, or by tapping into the collective unconscious and perceiving how present potentials are destined to manifest. In seminars, I have also directed participants to perceive the future with remote viewing techniques, but even the most renowned remote viewers now use the words *clairvoyant* and *remote viewing* interchangeably.

In the seminars, workshops, and research project, the hypnotized subjects mentally projected forward to New York City in time increments from 2000 to 2012. In each jump forward in time, they were to explore New York, then scan the rest of the world, before returning to explore conditions in the area in which they each lived. Each participant then filled out a report about the future they envisioned. The results of these explorations were reported in *Soaring Spirit* magazine #70, September 1998.

Several hundred people participated, and the predominant psychic observation was a changed New York skyline. A typical response was, "I see the Manhattan skyline changed. Part of the island is no longer there because of terrorist attacks and explosions." At least 10 percent of the respondents reported terrorism to come. Several people reported specifically on "Muslim terrorist attacks." Others talked about people walking through the streets of the city in snow that wasn't cold. This seems to be a clear reference to the ashes.

Was the attack on the World Trade Center a fated event?

Michael Drosnin, author of *The Bible Code* and *Bible Code II: The Countdown,* thinks so. Renowned Israeli mathematician Dr. Eliyahu Rips broke a code in the earliest edition of the Hebrew Bible and presented his work in a major science journal. The code, dating back 3,000 years, was confirmed by mathematicians around the world, including a senior code-breaker at the top secret U.S. National Security Agency. Upon hearing about the code, Drosnin, a former reporter for the *Wall Street Journal* and the *Washington Post,* began a five-year investigation. The code predicted both Kennedy assassinations, the Oklahoma City bombing, the moon landing, and everything from World War II to Watergate, and from the Holocaust to Hiroshima.

Drosnin discovered that the Bible code even predicted the assassination of Yitzhak Rabin. He personally warned the prime minister of the conditions surrounding the slaying. The warning was disregarded, and the assassination happened, as predicted, when predicted.

On September 11, 2001, Drosnin was awakened by the sound of the first jumbo jet exploding into the World Trade Center. He ran up to the roof of his Lower Manhattan apartment building just in time to see the second plane fly into the second tower. He watched as the towers collapsed. "My mind could not take in the scale of the destruction my eyes had seen. It was on a scale only captured in biblical prophecy.

"I ran down from the roof and immediately searched the ancient code on my computer, the Bible code. It was the one place I might find confirmation of the full danger and a revelation of what was yet to come."

Drosnin quickly found that "twin towers" was encoded by the word "airplane." Crossing those words in the text was the message, "It caused to fall, knocked down." These were coded words from 3,000 years before. The author discovered other related encryption including, "Sin, crime of Bin Laden," "They saw smoke rising above the land like the smoke of a furnace," "Terrorist Atta," and "Egyptian man."

Mohammed Atta was the pilot of the first plane to hit the towers.

Moving from fact to fiction, in his book *Illusions,* Richard Bach talks about life as a movie. Reluctant Messiah Donald Shimoda says, ". . . the world's best movie is still an illusion, is it not? The pictures aren't even moving, they only appear to move." A movie is like a lifetime, but Richard wonders why anyone would attend a horror film. Shimoda explains that those attending feel they deserve to be horrified—to be unhappy.

"You can hold a reel of film in your hands, and it's all finished and complete—beginning, middle, end are all there that same second, the same millionths of a second. The film exists beyond the time that it records, and if you know what the movie is, you know generally what's going to happen before you walk into the theater; there's going to be battles and excitement, winners and losers, romance, disaster; you know that's all going to be there. But in order to get caught up and swept away in it, in order to enjoy it to its most, you have to put it in a projector and let it go through the lens minute by minute . . . any illusion requires space and time to be experienced. So you pay your nickel and you get your ticket and you settle down and forget what's going on outside the theater and the movie begins for you."

Maybe we're all watching a movie that was written, produced, directed, and filmed a long time ago. Maybe in the instant our source created the spark that created the universe, everything was destined to be.

Maybe.

When Einstein came up with the equation $E=mc^2$, he informed the world that matter is energy. The scientific community quickly verified his findings. This means that all the metal, plastic, and wood surrounding you is not solid. What appears solid is actually made up of swirling molecules temporarily molded in their current patterns and vibrating at the rates of metal, plastic, and wood.

Everything on Earth, including the Earth itself, breaks down into subatomic particles, which means matter is energy. Our world and everything in it is not what it appears to be. Nothing is solid. Everything is energy. Your body is energy . . . and *energy is nonphysical in nature.*

Cutting-edge physicists are now saying our reality appears to be more like a "thought form" than anything else. This fact does not surprise the mystics who always said we live in a world of illusion.

Here we are vibrating within a particular range. Imagine a radio dial. We're at 99.5 but there may be another reality at 101.2 and another at 103.6. Think of how many audio programs are flowing through your room right now. With a radio, you can listen to one after another. Einstein and many other scientists believe different realities coexist in the same space on different frequencies, just as the different stations play in the same space at the same time.

In the early 1970s, I studied informally with Navajo shaman David Paladin. David was an acclaimed artist and a student of all things mystical. He said that depending upon the circumstances, we can exist in more than one frequency at one time. "I died last night," he once told me. "I had a heart attack in another reality, and Lynda and the children are mourning me. But I'm still here interacting with them in this reality."

Maybe the World Trade Center is still standing in another frequency of time and space? Maybe the people who died in the airplanes crashed by terrorists are still alive in another reality?

The idea of a group of people being drawn together for a rendezvous with death captivated me as a teenager upon reading a 1957 book titled *Many Wonderful Things* by Robert W. Huffman and Irene Specht. The book described a series of hypnotic experiments carried out over a period of two years. The authors felt they had uncovered evidence that man has a "third" mind—a God mind—a part of God within the self. Much of the book consists of questions asked of a deeply hypnotized subject who responds with enlightened answers.

When asked if an airline crash is destined, the subject says, "The passengers have created this situation, this learning, this understanding, through their own learning and mistakes. But we make death a horror, a fear, a punishment . . . no, no! It is a true and joyous release . . . and resting time."

The hypnotized subject goes on to explain, "They [the passengers] would be drawn together to learn together. But God does not predetermine these things. We have done so by our mistakes, our errors, our learning."

If this is so, were the events, mistakes, or learning requirements that caused people to board the September 11 airplanes actually set in motion thousands of years ago?

Fate is a destiny created by oneself, which is inevitable and unavoidable, due to one's own karma. Karma is the principle that makes you the cause of all your life circumstances, resulting from your past activities, thoughts, and emotions throughout all your incarnations.

In looking at karma, Dharma, and destiny, Mahatma Gandhi used the analogy of a card game. Your karma is the hand of cards you're dealt. Your Dharma is how you play the cards. Dharma is commonly considered to be your duty to self and to society. One set of cards appears to be luckier than another set. This would be determined by the karma the person has earned and wants to work on.

A common view of predestination says the river of life is carrying us in a particular direction. We can swim over to the left bank, or to the right, or we can catch the swifter current in the middle of the river. We can even decide to fight the flow and swim back upstream for awhile. But eventually, we're going to end up in the sea.

Another view states that the free will of today is the determinism of tomorrow. Let's say you go to the airport and hundreds of destinations are available to you. You have the free will to choose where you want to go. Once you decide on Los Angeles, buy your ticket, and board the plane, you'll end up in Los Angeles. You'll then have to accept the consequences of your decision.

More than one astrologer has told me, "We live our lives day to day as if we had choices. We choose to do this or do that, while all the time, the outcome has already been determined. Fate will intervene to assure we end up where we are destined to be, doing what we're destined to be doing, with whom we're destined to be with."

And the purpose of reincarnating over and over again, playing this game of life over and over again, is to attain a higher state of consciousness. With that goal in mind, I will share the story of a reporter who once asked Maharishi Mahesh Yogi, "How does the world look in the highest state of consciousness?"

"You see that everything is *exactly* as it should be," said Maharishi.

The reporter hesitated before asking, "But why then are you working so hard to improve the situation?"

Maharishi smiled. "Because that is *exactly* as it should be."

2

Tara Sutphen's Soul Contract

"[W]e will be guided to be in the right place at exactly the right time and to meet the people we need to encounter."
—Bob Frissell, American author

Jess Stearn, author of *The Sleeping Prophet* and other New Age books, wrote a chapter about Tara and me in his book *Soulmates*. I have also told our story in my book *Earthly Purpose*, as well as in numerous print and website articles. Rather than repeat myself here, I'll simply share a few paragraphs about our initial meeting from *Earthly Purpose*, followed by one of my "Master of Life" Web columns.

On the night of February 19, 1983, the house was full of exciting people—the party was a definite success. I had just walked into the kitchen to refill my drink when I spotted Jess Stearn making his way through the crowd. He was accompanied by a couple of his male friends and a black-haired, emerald-eyed, lean and lovely young woman.

My throat contracted, and I could hardly breathe. She was the most beautiful woman I'd ever seen. She was dressed in a red western shirt, skintight black jeans, and red cowboy boots. "Richard," Jess said, "this is Tara McKean. She's visiting from Sedro Woolley, Washington."

"Hi," she said shyly.

Tara's smiling eyes hid a sensuous flame that crackled above the sounds of the party. There was no one else in the room. There had never been anyone else. "I'm glad you could come," I said, a faint tremor in my voice, as though some deep, long-forgotten emotion had been touched.

Tara offered to get Jess a drink. Halfway across the kitchen she turned to look at me—a look that will linger forever in my mind, a look that will probably flash before my inner eyes for incarnations to come, a look of recognition and confusion that reflected everything I was feeling. If I had listened, I would probably have heard the voices of our spirit guides echoing across the universe, congratulating each other on a masterful job of maneuvering.

Tara and I have been together since shortly after we met—21 years as I write these words. In 1983, she had a six-year-old son, and I had a five-year-old son, both from previous marriages. We established our home in Malibu, California, and our children became the best of friends. As an established New Age author, I conducted metaphysical seminars all over the country. Tara accompanied me on the road and enjoyed participating in psychic sessions such as automatic writing and telepathy. While automatic writing, she made contact with her spirit guide, Abenda, who predicted future events. The predictions came true, over and over again, including the prediction that Tara and I would have two children of our own.

My wife decided to train with leading professionals in palmistry and astrology. She was soon combining Eastern and Western forms of astrology in ways I had never seen done before. And the accuracy of this unique charting was undeniable. With a natural talent for all things psychic, Tara devoted herself to mastering the esoteric sciences and continues to study, explore, and experiment to this day.

I wrote the following Web column in 2003 in response to some of Tara's automatic writing:

> I am stuck on the number of incarnations it takes to get from A to Z.
>
> "Nobody is doing anything new. All that you are doing now you have done so many times, so many *million* times. It is nothing new. This anger, this greed, this sex, this ambition, this possessiveness—you have done it all millions of times," says Osho, the East Indian guru.
>
> Millions?
>
> I have a problem with millions. As someone who communicates a lot on the subject of reincarnation, I have been regressed dozens of times. And Tara's spirit guide, Abenda, has told me of many additional incarnations. So I am probably aware of about 50 lifetimes. Were I to experience more past-life regressions, additional incarnations would probably surface.
>
> The Buddhists say it takes about 600 lifetimes to finally attain enlightenment and a level of consciousness that can free you from the need to return to the physical world.
>
> Six hundred is a long way from millions.
>
> I decided to have Tara ask Abenda about this during one of her automatic writing sessions. This is what her spirit guide wrote to me: "Richard, you have had 53,042 lifetimes upon the Earth. You have had more in other galaxy systems."
>
> "Oh, come on! Fifty-three thousand forty-two is ridiculous," I said upon reading the words aloud. For a moment, I feared that everyone else managed to pull it off in about 600 lifetimes, and that I must be a very slow learner.
>
> There was more writing: "In almost all of the lifetimes, you come back with other loved ones. There have been a few lifetimes where you came in alone, but usually you are followed in, so that your courage and bravado might be buffered. You have had 18,003 lifetimes with Tara in various groups and family situations. You two have been partners or mates 13,552 of

those lifetimes. You only recall the most vivid or the most beautiful."

"You think we'd be sick of each other," I said upon reading this. "I'm still upset about the Mongolian lifetime in which you were the man and I was a woman, and you left me and the children to ride off on your horse and fight. What would we find if we explored 13,551 more incarnations?"

Tara had no problem with the numbers. I did. Planet Earth would have had to eliminate all traces of countless numbers of civilizations for this to be valid. Atlantis and Lemuria would be like yesterday when compared to the length of the timeline.

Discoveries supportive of a longer timeline certainly exist. A glazed wall uncovered by coal miners hundreds of feet below the surface—a wall that continued and was found in another coal mine miles away. In a different location, miners discovered a beautifully crafted silver teapot in coal dating back to the days of dinosaurs. Brad Steiger wrote of many such documented finds in his book *Worlds before Our Own*.

Fifty-three thousand forty-two lifetimes? Maybe. I've decided not to dwell on it.

If Tara's automatic writing had not been so accurate over the years, I would not take such communications seriously. One could argue that because we knew of the predictions, we manifested outcomes as self-fulfilling prophecy. But often they foretold events related to other people who were well beyond our ability to influence.

While I am awed by accurate predictions and astrology readings that reflect your life like a mirror, Tara sees such things as a natural unfolding of life. "As a young child, I knew of my past lives," she said. "My father often rocked me to sleep in response to nightmares in which the Germans were coming for me during World War II. Eventually I was captured and gassed in the concentration-camp showers.

"At eight years of age, I nearly bled to death from a bicycle accident. While floating above the operating table, I perceived a joyous and comforting light and began to rush toward it. But two women walked up to me, blocking my way to the source of the light. They bent down and told me their names were Abenda and Francoise. They talked to me about my life and family before telling me it was time to go back. I didn't want to go back, but soon experienced myself floating over my body again. The next thing I remembered was waking up in the hospital ward.

"Francoise was my spirit guide until my early twenties, when Abenda stepped in to take over. It was at this time I began to experiment with automatic writing. Today, Abenda is like a member of our family, although my brothers still call her my 'imaginary friend.' But the moment anyone needs advice or must make an important decision, guess who they ask me to contact? That's right. Abenda."

In seeking to understand this unique association with her spirit guide, Tara claims it is based upon a soul contract they agreed upon before Tara was born. "At first, my automatic-writing communications with Abenda were primarily about family and friends, all of whom encouraged me to keep at it, because the predictions in the writing turned out to be so accurate," Tara said. "In 1991 I began to write a 'Cause and Effect' column in our *Soaring Spirit* magazine. People with problems sent me questions about their lives and Abenda chose the letters she felt would best relate to the rest of our readers. To receive the communications, I go into a theta-level altered state of consciousness, and Abenda finds someone on the Other Side who knows the letter writer or a loving entity who is aware of the problem. Under my spirit guide's carefully orchestrated conditions, this soul controls my hand and the response is received via automatic writing.

"The answers I receive explain the letter writer's karma—the past-life reasons for current problems. Soon after the column began running, I started to receive verifications from the writers, assuring me and my readers that I was indeed in communication with souls and that I was providing valid information."

In 2003, Ft. Lauderdale hypnotherapist Dan Cleary asked Tara to explain her automatic-writing technique in *The Link,* a magazine for professional hypnotherapists.

> Upon attaining my trance level, I visualize myself in the center of a Celtic stone circle. I feel the grass beneath my bare feet,

and I look upon the stone altar. I place a symbolic gift upon the altar (flowers, stones, or feathers) and I chant a blessing for my Earth life. Then I leave the circle, feeling the Earth and grass as I run, and feel myself running until I am flying out of Earth's atmosphere. In time, I come to a white mist where I find stairs ascending up into the mist. The stairs are ancient, gray, and worn. I reach out and touch the surface. My deceased Grandmother Gwendolyn is often waiting at the bottom of the stairs to give me a bouquet of flowers. She refuses to ascend to a higher level until her children cross over.

Focusing my senses, I feel myself walking up the stairs, going higher and higher, until I come to a landing where Abenda awaits in the doorway to my temple room. Abenda and I hug upon meeting and then enter the room together, which is furnished with unusual furniture I'm told is Persian. Yellow Chinese silk pillows abound, and East Indian statuary accents the decor. In my Earthly reality, I love Native American, Western, and Spanish decor, but I am very comfortable here and can see, touch, even smell the room. I feel an almost complete transference of energy. My physical body is numb, and I no longer hear or see what is going on in my real life.

My temple-room time becomes my reality while I am there. I scrunch pillows to relax on the couch while conversing with Abenda. Over the years, she's learned to joke and play with me. That took awhile, because she perceives our association as a working relationship, and she wants to keep the energy between us clear and precise. We get into intense conversations, and we can even have arguments. Some of the disagreements relate to work versus play. Abenda doesn't live an Earthly life. She died brutally in her last incarnation and wants no association with our physical world other than to help us through our Earthly trials and tribulations.

When I'm channeling for an individual who has written to me about a problem, I physically hold their letter or another touchstone, such as a lock of hair or a photograph. Still deep in trance, I visualize myself strolling out the back door of my temple room and going to a glass teahouse. In this separate environment, Abenda calls in the letter writer's spirit guide or someone on the other side who loves them through a past-life connection. I perceive this soul, who has come to write through me, just as if they were actually sitting beside me here on Earth. Usually, they come to communicate wearing what they wore in the past life they shared with the letter writer. If they were shy and demure in a past life, they will appear the same today. A flamboyant man from a 1700s incarnation will still be showy when he walks into the teahouse to communicate.

Abenda has to provide an "okay" for an entity to write through my hand. Anyone from a lower vibration is not allowed contact. She also stresses that the contact must use the English language. If they have difficulty writing legibly, they can allow me to use my own handwriting.

To better explain this process of questions and answers between Tara and those in spirit, the following are examples of the communications, originally published in her "Cause & Effect" column.

Letter from Marianne Pflanz of Armond Beach, Florida: My youngest son, Sean, 24, was killed in September while riding a bicycle on a rainy night. We were very close. Although I accept the concepts of reincarnation and karma, it is hard to apply these beliefs to someone I love and miss terribly.

At his grave, I did a psychometry reading: I saw the drunken driver playing tag with my son. Then I saw hundreds of bikes, and Sean gave me a huge wave like he was starting up to race. He had a big smile on his face. Then he got serious and rode off a cliff into the clouds. I doubt the validity of this. I have joined bereavement groups. Is there anything you can tell me that will help me to find peace?

Tara's response: Your son Sean and Justine Melbourne both came to me to write their responses to your question. Justine provided the first message: "Sean will always love you and the family. He is every day in your thoughts, he knows this and wishes you all well. He's sorry to have caused so much pain and sadness, but he wants you to know he had to go—his time in this incarnation was over and he hopes he touched your lives in a good way. He wanted to be reckless and free to have some fun—some laughs— to live a real life as he had lived such a bad life in his previous incarnation as a prisoner of war during World War II.

"Sean needed to go because he will reincarnate next year in a nice family in southern Illinois. Your son has political aspirations, and in his next life he will have to be serious and conscientious, for politics will change greatly in the next century. He will be powerful, brave, and courageous and in your hearts you will be proud of him. The short, good life he led with you will allow him to be stronger in the future.

"Send him beautiful thoughts. He receives every one and loves them. Try not to be sad, for this makes Sean feel sad. I am here to console you and the family. Your present family was once incarnated together as Indians in the fifteenth century in what is now Wyoming. This was a happy time, and subconsciously you all remember it."

Sean writes: "I wish to say to my mother and my family that I did not mean to hurt any of them. And in no way would I have died in the way I did if I had been more conscious of my family's feelings. I simply chose a fun way to go. I'm sorry I felt biking was fun, but you all know I did. So you must know it was a recreational death. I couldn't have asked for a better family this time. And I am sorry to all of you for all the times I was uncaring and had bad manners. I was rude a lot, and I know I was consciously trying to make my own transition easier by trying not to care so much. But your caring has touched me deeply, and I hope to touch your lives when you are old and need me more to help the world become a better place. Be strong. Be the same family I knew and loved. Please! Love to you all, Sean."

Letter from a Grand Haven, Michigan, reader who asked that her name be withheld: I married an angel-gone-bad: a very talented, but dark and cruel man. Our marriage ended in divorce, financial loss, career crisis, and my broken heart. I was a notch above despair only because our beautiful daughter had been spared his dark side, or so I thought. A year ago, she attempted suicide and was found to be a chronic alcoholic at age

15. She revealed to me that both her father and paternal grandfather had been molesting her.

Is it karma? I am learning to make better choices, but maybe my lifelong vision of myself as strong, confident, and a healer is a delusion. My daughter is nearly 12 months clean and sober, and she has a strong will to live. Any wisdom or insight you can provide, no matter how painful, will be most welcome.

Tara's response: A man named Bramaha, large, dark complexioned, with a full beard, came to write through my hand. "You chose to return to this man in this life as you were his love in the Sudan—a beautiful harem girl who loved him very much. Although he had many lovers, he cared for you. He felt it was his right to have anyone and anything he wanted, including sex with his many daughters. Today, he continues this sexual pattern. His current-life moral code has not changed. It is too bad he is not seeing a hypnotherapist, for if he knew the source of the problem, maybe he could bring himself back into balance. He never meant harm, but has been blind to his hunger for satisfaction and the pain it has caused. He will have to learn through the pain of being molested himself in a future time.

"You have incarnated to be with him many times, but now the anger is strong. You must release this negative energy or it will assure another future union with him. Search your heart for forgiveness. In other times, you, too, have been the perpetrator of suffering.

"Your daughter will be fine when she has had time to access her feelings and come to terms with what has happened. You do not need to hover over her in fear. She needs you and you accept your responsibility. Be a source of support, fun, and camaraderie. The bond you share is good and will help to carry you through all trying tests. She is also testing your love from another shared lifetime. You left her in a past life—gave her away at birth. You did not care what happened to her. But in this life, she has found a way to make sure that you cared about her. In doing so, she took steps she didn't realize would be so difficult. You will both work it out. Forgiveness is the key to karmic evolution."

Abenda came to me to add this note: "Yes, the situation is

karmic. On a spiritual level, you accepted this experience for the balance it offered you and your daughter. Another way to look at this: you accepted the role of mother lion ready to save your child. It is your duty to your daughter. You will survive, and it will be over when you purge yourself of the repugnant emotions currently permeating your mind. When you do, you break the tie with your husband and in the future he will have to find someone with karma matching his needs. Work at believing in yourself as a good mother, provider, and teacher. No matter what else happens, you now gain confidence in your actions. In oneness, Abenda."

Letter from Gerald Hendrickson of Kentwood, Michigan: My mother once told me that when I was one hour old, I stared up at her in a "challenging way." As a result, she says she treated me differently than my brothers and sisters. I'm now 62, and I continue to wonder how a newborn baby can challenge anybody.

I was widowed in 1984 after 16 years of marriage. Our daughter was 14 at the time. I had quite a time raising her. She felt that her mother's death didn't affect anyone but her. About this time I developed Crohn's disease, which is hard to deal with since it affects the entire digestive system from one end to the other. I wonder what I did in a previous life to cause this kind of karma.

Tara's response: Reginald Frankan came to write to you saying, "Although originally Frenchmen, you, Gerald, and I were explorers together in Tehran in the eighteenth century.

"Your mother wasn't challenged by you when you were born. Her life was one of continued depression, and she was very weak and alone all that time. Even though she had people around her, she felt no connection to anyone.

"This life relates back to the 1500s in a remote area of Sweden. You and your mother in your current life were then twin younger brothers in a family that included a stern older brother, older sisters, and a stern father. Your mother died in childbirth, and the twins were blamed for killing her. This was the karmic plan, and as a result, you two twins became allies in your remote world. The family was unloving, uncaring, and resentful. You two were dutiful and if not loving, you did carry your responsibilities well.

"When fever broke out, all died but the two of you and two sisters. The sisters were used to being told what to do, so you assumed the dominant role. You blossomed in this position, but your brother resented the fact you were becoming like your father and older brother. He decided to leave and join an army passing by. You never saw each other again.

"Before he died in the army, he swore that he would never follow you again. He loved you too much to be near you and didn't trust that you weren't like the others. You waited in vain for his return during that life.

"This life, you followed him. He, as your mother, had asked you prior to your birth not to join her in this life, because she was using the incarnation to clear up some undesirable karma. She wanted to reestablish a long, loving relationship and friendship with you, but this wasn't the life to do that. On a subconscious level she was angry that you incarnated to be with her, but it wasn't because she didn't love you. She loved you too much. She needed to suffer. She didn't want you to suffer. Her anger was toward the energy surrounding her own karmic destiny.

"She wished to die, but she had to linger many years. This was very hard on you, and the health problems you have are related to being unable to let go of your guilt and anger.

"You need to create peace with your mother and your departed wife. Your wife was sad to leave your daughter, but your daughter had left her before in many lifetimes—in 1791 on the steps of a Roman church. She had been too poor to raise the child, but the child missed her mother all her life nonetheless. You were the priest who saved the child. In their next shared incarnation, your wife and daughter will be devoted to one another with no more karma to work out.

"Your current health problems can be helped much more in this life. Continue to seek therapy—there are remedies for you. You hold on to your life, your way of life, and those you love out of fear. As a result, this condition has surfaced. You need to trust the universe and your karma. Know that you can be worry free and still be in control of your fate. Your friend, Reginald."

In 1997, after answering letters like those above, Tara continued her automatic writing by questioning Abenda about the influence of earthly astrological factors after a soul has crossed over into spirit. Abenda responded by writing, "Since I have not reincarnated with new aspects, my last lifetime affects me still."

Tara asked for Abenda's past-life astrological information. "She didn't hesitate to tell me. She was born April 24, 1814, at 3:12 A.M., in Alban, France. And she reminded me that I was her mother in that incarnation. When I combined my astrological chart with hers, the astrology reflects the relationship we share today."

My wife began searching out family-to-family French history on the Web. This quest was fueled by Abenda providing Tara with family names and information in dreams. Upon awakening in the morning, Tara would rush to her computer to see if the new information was traceable. Often it was. Our son Hunter, age 12 at the time, claimed, "Mom is obsessed with dead French people."

After conducting workshops at the Mind Body Spirit Festival in London, England, during the summer of 1998, Tara and I took a ten-day research trip through French towns and graveyards. We tracked Abenda's last life, found related family history, and walked through miles of gravestones.

The biggest surprise of the trip came when we visited the town of Albi, one town away from Abenda's birthplace of Alban. Arriving late in the afternoon, we checked into a beautiful hotel on a river running through the town. At dusk, we walked hand-in-hand across a long bridge over the water, into the town, and through the surrounding countryside. It was dark by the time we crossed the bridge back to the hotel."

"What was that?" I yelled in response to a ghostly illumination that suddenly descended and disappeared. I turned to Tara. Her eyes were wide, looking into the empty sky.

"You saw it, too?" she said, voice hopeful.

We were both familiar with Northern Lights, and this was not any Northern Light.

Tara squeezed my hand a little tighter, and we continued our walk across the bridge, only to be stopped again by a large apparition that seemed to illuminate the sky and a portion of the hotel before fading away. I spun around in hopes of seeing something that might be projecting the illusion. But with the exception of lights from the windows of homes on the far side of the river, there was only blackness. No moon even in the sky.

"Is Abenda saying 'Hello,' Tara?"

My wife shook her head.

Returning to the hotel, we sat in a grassy landscaped area and waited to see what would come next. The phenomenon repeated again and again. We remained outside for what seemed liked hours and never saw another guest. Being in the business we are in, we have had experiences that would cause most people's hair to stand straight up, but nothing relating to the spirit world ever seemed to rattle my wife—until this. Tara said, "I have the feeling that when this is over something inexplicable will have transpired."

"Like what?"

"Like maybe we've stepped out of time and we're going to find that our children will have already grown old."

"Tara?"

"Or maybe we've crossed over and will soon be stepping into a brilliant light."

To this day, we do not know if anyone else saw this chimera light show. Tara speaks French and questioned hotel personnel about the phenomenon. They could not explain our experience and probably thought we had been drinking.

The ongoing Abenda research, as well as the individual case histories shared in this book, include astrological substantiation. Astrology assumes the interconnectedness of all things and is considered the first science. It was taught in universities until the 1600s, when "rational science" emerged. Tara uses Western astrology, which is based upon contemporary mathematical formulas relating to the movement of the planets, plus Eastern formulas dating back 2,000 years. She credits the teachings Alexander the Great brought from Chaldea as her primary Eastern influence when plotting a chart.

"In casting Abenda's astrological chart, I find she had a beautiful past life," Tara said. "She had friends, fulfillment, and beauty. There are several indications Abenda was very beautiful and bigger than life, possessing a lovable disposition. Her current radiant, positive energy may have been carried over from that life to continue to empower her in death.

"But the chart of the French incarnation also shows she was murdered. I know this from a past-life regression and from what she has told me. She was killed because she was a Vueiller (those who kept their tribal culture together) in the Second French Revolution. In 1850 she died in a town square as part of a public spectacle. Her chart shows she would be a martyr, dying for speaking out in support of the 'old ways.'

"A wealthy family is indicated, and she was surrounded by people who loved her. She probably married very well. Her husband thought the world of her, but I don't think she felt the same toward him. Her life was all about psychology, the occult, and exploring life's mysteries. Astrological configurations pushed her to speak out in her last life, and that aspect relates to our shared communications in this life.

"Abenda claims I was her mother in this French lifetime, and I think this relates back to my very first past-life regression with Jess Stearn—a couple years before Jess introduced me to Richard. In hypnosis, I regressed to a life as a mother of six children during this same period of French history."

To further clarify their relationship through astrological formulas, Tara combined her chart with Abenda's chart to come up with a new chart representing their union.

Tara and Abenda Composite Astrology: This chart shows our shared past life as mother and daughter was rich and fulfilling, but I died when Abenda was 16, and the loss was devastating for both of us. I died very suddenly—sick with a fever one minute and I was gone the next. We loved each other then as we do now. We've been in the same family in many incarnations. This is why she wanted to keep our connection in this lifetime. She wanted to be near me, but she is unwilling to come back to the Earth plane. She prefers to generate positive karma by helping me, so we established a soul contract to communicate in this way and share our awareness with others.

Our Sun is 25 degrees Aquarius—the sign of the future, future groups, futurists. The big thing is, of course, I can't see and know her in the flesh. That is shown in the first of the 12 astrological houses. The first house is about how you relate to life and present yourself to the world. I must have faith. Her influence is indicated here, which is true, and maybe I influence her as well.

On the Mercury—the planet of thinking and communications—it shows that we argue a little, and that is true. Yet we bring each other good things . . . and we're popular together talking. This seems to be the case, because people certainly seek us out and show interest in our work. It is our destiny to talk. And the chart shows that our popularity, our social standing, our benevolence, our messages in astrology, and the changes that come in life are from us speaking together. It shows that she will always be there for me.

Our most intense aspect is in the sixth house of work and career. It says that service to others will be more important than anything else we do together. We know that's true. It's all about higher knowledge and guidance. On the Midheaven—which indicates service to mankind—our relationship shows guidance. She is my guardian angel, there to guide me. Maybe I'm there to guide her, too.

Being married to Tara, I evidently share the responsibility of communicating the Abenda/Tara messages—or so my wife says. To substantiate this claim, Tara combined my astrology chart with Abenda's.

Dick and Abenda Combination Chart: Richard and Abenda have loved each other in a past life. It was a fortunate incarnation and the changes that occurred were intense. They might have even been married—maybe many times. There was definitely a lot of love between them, plus contracts, business, a lot of happiness, and social standing—all this is behind the scenes in their combined chart.

Although in spirit, Abenda still brings a happiness to

Richard. This shows they get along well. But there is a weird dynamic, probably because she is not on the Earth plane.

Their soul goal is to continue being there for each other and experience interaction, even though they live in separate worlds. They share extreme dedication, loyalty, and friendship, yet there's a feeling the relationship is somehow extravagant.

The biggest hurdles for Richard and Abenda have to do with the fact they reside in different realms. They may argue on the Other Side while Richard is out-of-body during sleep. She would prefer he followed safer paths through life, but he likes to walk a little closer to the edge, often generating controversy as a result. They go back and forth over that. Again and again, their chart depicts clever and piercing intellect applied to a very unusual relationship.

On their Midheaven is the most spiritual connection of all 360 degrees. She is in a spiritual position to support his communications, while he brings her into manifestation by sharing her truths through books, seminars, and on the Web. This is a very powerful and fortunate aspect.

She is there to help him in any sort of debate or daring action. If he were to feel melancholy or were having a problem, she'd want to be there emotionally for him. She wants to give him positive ideas in any way she can. Very unusual things come up on their Mercury—different kinds of communication skills. The Sun and Moon midpoint also indicates love and communication skills, which is usually a big hit in a relationship.

Their most intense aspect sits on faith, belief, trust, and liberty. Richard's Dharma—his duty to himself and society—is to liberate, which is a major part of Abenda's communications. In this life, they are associated through me to help people rise above their fear-based emotions—to cast away their delusions.

While Tara was charting all this astrology and going in and out of trance to question Abenda about her past life and the present connection they now shared, I asked my wife to question her spirit guide about predestination and how a prebirth planning session works. Tara received two communications via automatic writing:

Session 1: Everything you think, say, and do has an element of predestination inherent in the action. Prior to your birth you met with a council of advisors and elders. Your life was mapped out according to the karma you decided to resolve (the needed learning) and the good karma you wanted to experience (rewards). Your Dharma was factored in, and to use the analogy of a movie, you came to Earth to experience the script you wrote and agreed to play out.

Had you made every ideal choice, you would have experienced the movie exactly as it was scripted. But no one does that. Because you have free will, you can make a negative choice instead of a positive choice. Then the repercussions of each decision become a natural part of your movie.

Everyone incarnates with their script in hand. The degree to which they stick to the script varies with each individual.

Maybe a better analogy would be the video games your son Hunter enjoys. Each game begins with several specific characters. If Hunter makes every move correctly, he speeds through the game to the top level. But initially that is impossible. So when he makes a wrong move, he proceeds down an alternate path that will have an outcome. The game has several preprogrammed alternate directions for every decision he makes. Some decisions lead to more jeopardy than others. Some decisions get his character killed. But each time he plays the game, Hunter learns a little better how to meet the tests he confronts and eventually he speeds through the game to the top level. This is very much how a soul scripts an Earth incarnation. If this can be so graphically demonstrated in a video game, is it difficult to imagine that your "game of life" could not be worked out with far more sophistication—with living, breathing characters?

Few souls know why they have come to Earth. Yet within their lineage of experiences lies the understanding, which can be perceived by anyone willing to do the inner work—sometimes extensive inner work (meditation, regression, research).

To truly live out your life experience, you must concentrate on the reality of Earth and bless the wonderment of what may be. But if you just focus on the ethereal side of existence, your life becomes ethereal and you may not fulfill your true physical purpose. Work, service to others, compassion, gaining knowledge, and finding love—these are some of the gifts Earth life offers. They are also pathways for a soul to advance.

But keep in mind that life on Earth is only a sub-life of your real life. You will one day return to the place you came from. For many centuries, I have studied the effects of reincarnation upon Earth lives. This is why the experimental relationship between Tara and me is so effective. Our current sharing was predetermined while Tara was on this side of the veil. Today, Tara can see and hear me. Few people are capable of this form of contact, but we have worked very hard to form this link so my messages can be easily perceived. If I were someone else's guide, I would give them messages in sleep and try to spark ideas intuitively. In times of trouble and pain, I would try to subconsciously provide comfort, instead of doing so directly, as with Tara.

Predestination brings you face-to-face with what you need to accomplish in this phase of existence. No matter what the situation, know that you choose the people, places, and things to experience the happiness and sorrow that will lead you to wisdom. You will not always get what you "think" you want, because you may have made other decisions when scripting your film. On a soul level, you're on a quest that takes priority.

Session 2: You are the creation of self, translated through energy waves within vibrational pattern alignments. Your ancient relative soul drives you to build a bigger and stronger lineage soul. You are like a tree with limbs. You can grow bigger and stronger and move toward the light when provided the right ingredients for evolution. While in spirit, within a schoolroom-like atmosphere, you choose karmic configurations matching your need to learn. It is up to you to do the homework and calculations, much like working on a science project. You create the blocks and focus the intensity factors that will manifest in your new incarnation. You can call in an overseer or two, but it is up to you to combine the elements to establish the life formula.

How well you thought it through will be known when your soul puts the life-plan into action. You receive counseling from the Elders and Masters once your life-plan is established. At that time the plan is easily read by the souls of your vibrational port. Their advice can help you avoid mistakes. If you take on more than you can handle, you may incur karma you did not anticipate. Once you go through the portal, you lose all perspective of who you are and who you once were. You become an Earthling with an agenda.[1]

3

Geri Jewell

"Free will allows you to be as happy or miserable as you desire to be, but you'll have to walk the path you laid out."
—Patty Conklin, American healer

1956, Buffalo, New York: Six months pregnant, Olga Jewell relaxed with her two young sons on the front porch of her home. She was enjoying the Indian summer afternoon and scanning the newspaper, when she looked up to see a speeding car leap the curb and careen across the lawn in her direction. Grabbing her sons, she dove for safety as the car smashed through the porch wall in a shatter of splintering wood and flying debris.

Although she saved herself and her sons from almost certain death, the fall caused Olga to hemorrhage. By the time she reached the hospital, her condition was critical. A priest performed last rites. The doctors pronounced the unborn baby dead and went to work to save Olga's life. When they realized the baby was alive, the child had been without oxygen for a critical period of time. Geraldine Ann Jewell was born three months premature with cerebral palsy (CP).

Fast forward 48 years to the present, and here is Geri's current press-kit copy: "Geri Jewell is known to millions as Cousin Geri from the NBC sitcom *The Facts of Life*. As the first person with a disability to become a regular performer on a national television show, she broke important new ground in a medium long hesitant in addressing issues of disability awareness."

The show ran from 1981 to 1984 and is still being rerun around the world. Geri went on to appear in lead roles in four major movies and guest starred in a dozen television shows. She played numerous roles in live theater and appeared as the opening act for stars such as Judy Collins, Paul Anka, and Robert Goulet. Her resume also highlights stand-up comedy appearances in over 600 clubs and regular motivational speaking engagements for Fortune 500 companies.

Tara and I met Geri's younger sister, Gloria Elaine Jewell, in Sedona, Arizona, in August 2001. Gloria is a blue-eyed beauty with a bold, friendly personality. Over lunch we talked about her interest in metaphysics and her career as a top Realtor in Laguna Beach, California. I mentioned some research I was doing for a new book on karmic destiny. Gloria said her sister Geri might make a good case history, because she was born with a disability but had overcome it on a grand scale. "She's really a teacher," Gloria said. "She educates people about disabilities in a way they can understand and accept."

Over the months that followed, Gloria became a personal friend, and we set a date with Geri for an exploratory hypnosis session. If life is karmically preordained, why would Geri decide to be born with a disability and then use it to launch a career that served all disabled people? It was a question I hoped past-life regression could help answer.

Geri is a delightful mix of pixieish energy, lots of enthusiasm, and a huge smile that melts your heart. You quickly realize that she's going to drop a punch line into any lingering attempt to be serious. Geri has difficulty controlling some movements, is hearing impaired, and relies to some extent upon lip reading. But minutes after meeting her, your awareness of her CP condition fades into the background.

We decided to conduct the past-life regression in the living room of Gloria's house in the hills above Laguna Beach. Tara agreed to monitor the session. A monitor mentally connects to the subject and goes into hypnosis along with them. If successful, the monitor perceives what the subject is experiencing in regression. It's not unusual for a monitor to perceive images before the subject verbalizes an experience. On occasion, a good monitor also picks up on related lifetimes being subconsciously avoided because the memories are painful.

Psychic monitoring isn't a hard science. A successful session depends on the psychic talents of the monitor and/or the brainwave compatibility of the two people. A chakra link is established as part of the hypnotic induction to intensify the connection between the monitor and the regression subject. This is a matter of having both people visually link the top four of the seven chakra-energy centers in the human body.

They imagine a purple light emerging from their crown chakra on the top of their head, and it arches up, across and over, connecting with the other person's crown chakra. This is followed by an indigo-blue light connecting third-eye brow chakras, a silvery-blue light connecting throat chakras, and a golden light connecting heart chakras. Although this may sound like an implausible exercise, I have conducted many kinds of psychic sessions both with and without the dual chakra link. The chakra link always increases telepathic accuracy, or as used between Tara and Geri, allows the psychic monitor to better perceive what the regression subject is experiencing.

After directing a full body relaxation, I directed a Tara/Geri chakra link and induced a deep hypnotic sleep. When the induction was complete, I said, "In the memory banks of your subconscious mind there's a memory of everything you've ever experienced in this life you're now living and in all of your past lives. Every thought, word, and deed is recorded, and it's now time to bring forgotten awareness to the surface so that you may better understand what influences, restricts, or motivates you in the present. And I'd like you to go back to a lifetime that will help us to understand why you were born with cerebral palsy. There may be many lifetimes that relate to your condition, but let's begin our exploration with an important incarnation."

Upon completing the transfer in time, I said, "Speak up and tell me what you see and what you're doing."

Geri: "There's a pyramid . . . a lot of tunnels."

"Are you in one of the tunnels?"

Geri: "Yes, there's a smell."

"Are there others in the tunnels with you?"

Geri: "There are others outside . . . a lot of people. I'm very small. I can fit where others can't. I'm trying to find something. Knowledge."

"Let's move ahead until you find what you're seeking or until something happens. On the count of three you'll be there—one, two, three."

Geri: "There's a bright light coming from somewhere. I can see writing, there's writing. But I can't get out. Oh-h-h-h."

"Why can't you get out?"

Geri: "Trapped. I can't bring back what I'm supposed to bring back. They're trying to get me out, but they can't."

"What is happening? What are you feeling?"

Geri: "Pain. Crushed."

"Did you spring a trap built into the pyramid? Has something fallen on you?"

Geri: "Yes."

Geri became emotional and said she was no longer there. I assumed this to mean she had left her body and crossed over into spirit, so I gave her suggestions to return to the present, so I could direct her up into a Higher Self level of mind.

The moment Geri began to speak about the pyramids, Tara began writing:

"Egypt. Raiding the tombs. He is a small man working for the British. He shouldn't have gone in, because he feared he was violating the curse of the Pharaohs. He knew it was a mistake, but his family needed money. He chose to be a small man in this incarnation to avoid having stature."

While I was directing Geri to transcend levels of consciousness by moving up into Higher Self, Tara began writing about Rome. "A previous incarnation in Rome. A gladiator who kills many people for sport. So strong and yet so sensitive. Sometimes he cries at night. He knows it is wrong, but he is in service to the Caesar. He eventually dies by a sword being driven through his stomach.

"A soul decision is made to resolve the guilt. In future incarnations, this soul will experience introverted positions. If weak, the soul can't shine and be arrogant through displays of strength and brutality. Geri accepts Buddha's law of serving others until you can do no more. Your sacrifice will set you free. She is still seeking knowledge, but the knowledge is outwardly unattainable. She finds the knowledge through self-sacrifice and humility."

Hypnotherapists and brain/mind researchers generally accept the notion that we use only ten percent of our mind. You're familiar with conscious mind. Your subconscious mind is a memory bank, and your superconscious mind is often called Higher Self by metaphysicians. Higher Self lies within the 90 percent of our minds we do not normally use. At this level you find psychic abilities and an awareness of your totality, including a doorway to what Carl Jung referred to as the Collective Unconscious—the total awareness of mankind.

I like to take my subjects to this level after some initial past-life explorations, because in Higher Self we can attain information faster. Not only can my subject access the information recorded in the subconscious mind, he or she can provide an overview of their life plan, karmic goals, soul associations, and soul contracts.

Once Geri was in Higher Self, I began to ask questions: "Geri, tell me about your life plan."

Geri: "I came to be a teacher."

"Why did you take on this Dharma?"

Geri: "Because I'm strong. Coming into this life as I am is as normal to me as your body is to you. The only thing that makes it different is how I'm being perceived by others. If left alone, if never told that I have this, I wouldn't have known that I did. I'm to teach others that they can do the same things I've done and more. We're only as limited as we allow ourselves to be. But CP has also taught me humility."

"Was learning humility part of your karmic plan, and if so, why?"

Geri: "Rome. I'm always a male. I was very powerful, very wealthy, but I don't appreciate . . . I see myself strong . . . armor. Oh-h-h-h-h, I can't go there." At this point Geri became emotional again.

"Be relaxed and at ease. Breathe deeply and let go of all the emotion" (pause). "Can you tell me how the past life in the pyramid tunnel relates to this life?"

Geri: "I sought the knowledge but didn't attain it."

"You thought the knowledge was in the pyramid?"

Geri: "That's exactly what it was, but now I'm attaining the knowledge without the pyramids. I don't know if it was the writing, but something was within the pyramids that could have taught me what I'm learning now. It's through my disability that I've acquired my spirituality. Without it, I would have been like I was in Rome. I can still shine without being so arrogant and insensitive to all people. The problem . . . the biggest hurdle is still arrogance. In one life I was retarded. I was a girl. It was an important life."

"How was it important?"

Geri: "I experienced kindness and being protected. My current life is harder, because I understand. In that life I was separate from the rest of society. Then, I didn't understand. But now I understand."

"Did that life set up the CP condition in this life?"

Geri: "Yes, oh, absolutely. I think that because I move the way I do, people think that I'm retarded. So I feel very strongly connected to that life, because they're somewhat the same."

"But why did you need your current life to be an extension of that life?"

Geri: "In that life, with mental retardation I couldn't help other people. I was unable to have a voice. The karma was just for myself and the people around me, mainly my parents. This time, I wanted to come back to unify. And I had to make peace with so many different things. I had to let go of my prejudices from many lifetimes. That was the only way I could take it to another level and do the work I do."

"Okay, let me ask you something else. Was your sister Gloria involved with you in any of these past lives?"

Geri: "Gloria and I have been together many times. She was with me in Rome. She was my mother."

"Why did you come back together in this life?"

Geri: "We needed each other. We balance each other. She's made me strong. If Gloria could do something, I could do it, too."

While Geri was responding to my questions in Higher Self, Tara was writing the following: "Geri wants to be protected as she seeks 'the Grail'—knowledge, power, and self-respect. She is reaching understanding and the knowledge she seeks will release her suffering and allow her to attain enlightenment. This enlightenment will allow her to forgive herself. She no longer needs to suffer, and after this life, she will no longer punish herself. She will learn to love herself."

After the regression session, Tara showed us her writings on two of Geri's additional lifetimes since the Roman incarnation: "India. A disciple of Krishna. Very holy. She works in an orphanage and helps the poor. She is humble in this life while also seeking the energy of enlightenment.

"England. Royal court. She is the lady of a lord in 1751. She can't find an outlet for her pain. All her children have died at birth, and she is distraught after losing a tenth child. She does not love her husband anymore. He only thought it right to give her another chance at having a child, and she somehow blames him for giving her so many disappointments. She takes arsenic. She doesn't realize how much he cares for her until (from spirit) she experiences his terrible grief over her death. He hangs himself to follow her into death. She helps him cross to the light, where he remains a guide to this day. He isn't ready yet to live on the Earth, but he wants to help you. He also brings you sadness at times, because he has yet to rise above all the grief of that incarnation."

By the time we had finished the sessions, it was dusk. Sitting around a deck table, we tried to keep candles burning while a gentle breeze came in off the sea. Gloria served wine, cheese, meat, and fruit treats, plus homemade cookies. Below us, the lights of Laguna ran down to the sea, where fishing boats gathered to retrieve lobster pots.

Before I awakened Geri from the regression session, her spirit guide had encouraged her to write a book about her current life experiences. So I asked her about the viability of such a project.

"I've been putting it off," she said. "But I know it's time to start writing."

"Will you write a book?"

"Yes, I will."

A few days after the regression, Geri sent me an e-mail saying she had started doing Egyptian research on the Web. "Archaeologist Howard Carter discovered the tomb of King Tut," she said. "He described what it was like inside the pyramid. The steep staircases, the blocked passages, the hidden rooms. All this, I saw with you under hypnosis. Carter was determined to find ancient answers for the benefit of mankind. On November 26, 1922, he made a small opening, and discovered the tomb of King Tut. He also reported that when the opening was made, the light was almost blinding and he had to look away."

Was this a spiritual light or did it come from another source? Evidently Carter couldn't explain the light he experienced, and Geri could not explain the light she described in the pyramid tunnel.

In search of further substantiation of Geri's case history, Tara used her own unique combination of Eastern and Western astrology to read the past, analyze the present, and predict the future. The following excerpts are Tara's interpretation of aspects of Geri's birth chart illuminating her karmic pathway:

Geri's parents were very much in sync with each other when Geri was conceived and born. Her mother is the dominant parent and has played a major role in Geri's past lives as well. Geri's birth appears in the chart as a "predicament" (obviously the accident). Misfortune and unusual events surrounded her mother at the time: obstruction, damage, regrets, and worries about loss are all associated with the birth. But her parents very much wanted their baby to live.

The chart indicates that Geri has a quick wit and a sharp tongue, while also being courteous and refined. She has a lovable character with prophetic instincts. She worries a lot. Others see her as a communicator. She has natural acting ability, but suffers because her acting range is limited by CP. At the same time, status is indicated and her limitations have transformed her life in the area of career. Her communication skills generate money.

Much luck in career is indicated. Friends help her. Her intelligence and skills are applauded, and she is often surprised by how much she can influence others. She has notoriety and will always have an audience if she wants it.

Geri's Dharmic aspects (duty to self and society) sit on one of the royal Persian stars indicating honor, renown, and wealth. She was born to refocus herself, serve others, and experience love and friendship.

In summary: From a karmic perspective, nothing carries over from one life to the next like guilt. The guilt from the gladiator incarnation caused Geri to choose lives that minimized the potential of similar karmic mistakes. By assuming small stature in Egypt, she was no threat to others. The retarded female incarnation was a balancing and restful life offering no potential to harm. The incarnation as a Krishna disciple was a life of service, while the orphaned children may have provided an audience for her to entertain. Losing ten children in the English life was probably self-punishment to balance the lives taken in the Roman arena. In her current incarnation, Geri is again learning the humility that was lacking in the gladiator in the Roman arena.

As I write this, Geri is acting as a continuing character in a new HBO cable series titled *Deadwood*. She is also currently appearing on *The Young and the Restless* TV series. So again she has been drawn into the arena—this time the arena of national television, comedy clubs, and the speaking stage—all providing a greater understanding of those with disabilities.

4

Judi Chase

"Everything is fixed, all the transformations are fixed . . . The exact moment of gaining enlightenment is forever fixed."

—Maharishi Mahesh Yogi

June 6, 1995, Evergreen, Colorado: David Chase, 42, disappeared. Forty-seven days later, his nude body was recovered from Bear Creek. His neck had been broken, one hand had been nearly severed, and unusual abrasions were evident on his legs. The official cause of death was listed as drowning, but the case was investigated as a homicide.

David's widow, Judi, claimed her husband was murdered and made public accusations against a neighbor who was the last person to see David alive. Six months after this tragedy, Judi's two adoptive children were taken away under unusual circumstances. To Judi, these were not two separate tragedies, but one related tragedy.

Today, nine years later, thanks to Judi Chase's unrelenting

investigation, there is a better understanding of what happened and why. Judi is a tall, beautiful, brunette New Zealander with a smile that melts your heart. We first met years ago when Judi was booking speakers and workshop leaders for The Whole Life Expos—huge New Age festivals once popular in major cities. Our paths crossed again recently when Judi contacted me to do workshops for a scaled-down series of Body Mind & Spirit Expos. I enjoyed our phone conversations, which tended to go beyond talk about the New Age.

When I learned of her horrific experiences in the last few years, I asked if she would be willing to undergo past-life regression and some psychic investigation. We would try to find out why she had had to endure such pain. To me, only karma could provide the answer. Judi agreed.

Judi's male friend Dov, an accomplished New Age musician, accompanied her to the regression scheduled to take place in our Malibu home on a sunny March morning. Tara served coffee. Judi shared her story:

> I was married in February, 1993, on my husband David's fortieth birthday. We shared the dream of starting an orphanage for special-needs children. In 1994, we were able to actually start the orphanage in Evergreen, Colorado. It was to be a permanent home for drug babies. The twins, Tisha and Darius, born December 4, 1993, were the first adoptive children we brought into our lives.
>
> David was a cabinetmaker and when work was slow, he took on other projects. A neighbor asked David to help him with some roofing jobs. I asked my husband not to have anything to do with this guy, because the neighbor was the local drunk who had the lowest black energy I've ever experienced, and we got into a big fight over it.
>
> On June 6, 1995, David went with the neighbor to finish a roofing job and clear away brush at the Elks Club in nearby Morrison. The work was done by noon, and the two of them stopped at a local bank where David cashed an $1,800 check—an advance payment for cabinet work he was to start the following day. They then drank and shot pool at the Elks Club before

returning to Evergreen, where they continued the pool games at another bar called On the Rocks.

When David didn't return home that evening, Judi remained awake in her rocking chair until dawn. At first light, she drove to the neighbor's house and demanded to know where David was. He told her, "I left him in the bar shooting pool." When the police asked the same question, they were told that David had jumped into the river. That story was later altered to say that while throwing the debris from their truck into the river, David fell into the river.

Judi responded, "David would never have jumped into a snow-fed river. He was a seasoned mountain climber who knew the dangers of hypothermia. And as an environmentalist, he wouldn't throw so much as an apple core into the river, much less a truck full of debris. And if he had fallen into the river, the bar and local fire station were 50 yards away. A call for help could have saved David's life."

After four months of police investigation, little progress was made on the case. Then on October 15, 1995, retired police officer and private investigator Phil Harris had fallen asleep in his easy chair. He was awakened at 4 A.M. by a voice saying, "I'm David Chase. I was murdered. I want you to investigate my murder. Go buy the Sunday paper."

On page four of the paper, Phil found a story about Judi's attempts to resolve David's murder. Although he had never experienced anything like this before, the clairaudience (auditory psychic contact) and newspaper evidence convinced Phil that he was in contact with a dead man. He found the man's widow, Judi, and told her for a fee of $1, he would work the case until it was solved.

Judi explained, "When Phil contacted me, David had provided him with all kinds of insider information, pet names and other things that no one else could have known. I knew David was communicating with him."

David continued to provide Phil with information. From beyond the grave, he explained that the neighbor had talked him into cashing the check to buy a truck. That night, after hours of drinking, the two men got in a fight and David was hit in the back of the neck with a hard object that broke his neck. A knife was then used to cut the jeans from his body, the knife cutting into his skin, causing the abrasions. The $1,800 was stolen.

"Where is the murder suspect today?" I asked.

"The police have asked for his arrest and a half-million-dollar bail, but the D.A. won't prosecute because she doesn't have enough evidence yet to win a murder conviction. 'I have to convince 12 jurors beyond a reasonable doubt; otherwise the murderer will walk away and the case can never be tried again due to double jeopardy,' is what she told me," Judi said.

Judi claims to have worked with over 40 psychics and spiritual mediums in an attempt to help solve the case. The *Strange Universe* TV show put her together with James Van Praagh, who communicated with David on camera. Van Praagh described the details of David's death: "I see him being grabbed and hit . . . a blow to the back of the head. I see a lot of blood. Nobody came to help." The famous psychic also mentioned a dozen accurate events related to the murder and Judi's experiences in the aftermath.

"Will you tell us about losing the children, Judi?" I asked.

"A nanny was assigned to me by the adoption agency. Just one week after David disappeared, she arrived to live with me and help me complete the adoption. But the Department of Social Services (DSS) in Denver soon contacted me and said the kids had to be returned to their birth mother, who was now drug free. This is a risk you take in a situation like this. But I'd had the twins, Tisha and Darius, from the time of their birth, so I was heartbroken. I told DSS if the reunification plan failed, I wanted to complete the adoption.

"The DSS told me the twins would be placed in a local temporary foster home during the weekdays and live with their birth mother on weekends for the six-month trial period. Later I learned that my former nanny managed to become the temporary foster parent in Denver and she was also petitioning the courts to adopt the twins. The birth mom was only off drugs for six weeks. Whoever is holding children when parental rights are terminated has the first opportunity at adoption. The nanny and her mother were awarded the children before we even knew what happened."

"How did you find out that the twins had disappeared?" I asked.

"An investigator learned that the nanny never planned to adopt the children. She operated as a middleman for a third party in California. So the investigator provided the evidence to the district attorney, who reported it to the FBI. Agent Joe Schwecke was assigned to the case, but nothing has happened, primarily because Colorado seals adoption records."

Tears welled up in the corner of Judi's eyes. "I'm sorry," she said, taking a moment to grieve.

After allowing Judi time to regain her composure, I changed the subject to a discussion of how the past-life regression would be directed. When I asked if she was ready to begin, Judi took a deep breath, smiled faintly, and made herself comfortable on the couch. Once she was deep in hypnosis, I directed her to go back in time and explore why the dream she and David shared had become such a nightmare.

Judi: "I'm looking at the sky." Her voice was shaky.

"Look around and describe the environment."

Judi: "A castle in the background. Wind on my face. The ocean."

"Look down at your feet and tell me what you're wearing."

Judi: "A long dress."

"Is there anyone else here with you?"

Judi: "I'm alone."

"Does it feel good to be here? Are you at peace?"

Judi: "I'm trying to understand. I'm thinking about jumping off the cliff."

"Why are you upset?"

Judi: "I'm very upset, and I'm going to cry." She burst into deep sobbing tears. "I must have been so unhappy . . . so unhappy. I jumped."

I directed her away from the environment, gave her calming suggestions, and then moved her back in time to experience what had generated such despair.

She was a 17-year-old, at odds with her father, who had her locked her in her room (probably because she was pregnant, as we soon learn). "It's stone walls, an open window, cold. I'm just miserable." When asked where she lived, she responded, "Long grass. Dover."

"I want you to move in time to an important event," I said.

There was a long pause without a response. Throughout the induction and regression, Judi had not moved a muscle in her lower body, but she now seemed to be shifting uncomfortably in response to something she was mentally experiencing. "I'm giving birth to a baby. But . . . o-o-o-o-h."

She trembled, her fingers twitched nervously. "My baby's not here. My baby's not here." I gave her calming suggestions and asked her what had happened. "It's a bastard, so they took it away. I didn't even get to see it. My baby is gone." She became upset and began to cry again. "It was just too much for me. That's why I jumped."

I directed her to remember all she had experienced and to come back to the present while remaining in a deep altered state of consciousness. Once she was breathing normally, I guided her into Higher Self and asked for spirit guide assistance.

"Judi, in the past life when your child was taken away, you responded by jumping from the cliff. Because of that act, did you have to reincarnate and experience a similar situation again? This time your husband is murdered and two children are ripped away from you. Did you come back believing you would have the strength to pass the karmic test and go on with your life?"

Judi: "This is the truth. You know the truth."

After a pause, Judi began to speak with a staccato pacing that indicated she was channeling: "You know you're strong. You know how to walk through fire, overcome all obstacles. Never give up. Follow your intuition, your inner wisdom. Speak of truth and justice. You will not fail. You cannot fail, for you're a warrior soul. You have work to do. You will not lose your life. And you will make sure that good prevails over evil. Justice is the order of the day, and the little ones are protected. They are in your hands. This is all ordained."

"Who was speaking through you, Judi?"

Judi: "My Higher Self."

"All right, I'd like you to perceive a karmic overview of your relationship with David and all that has happened. You found each other, shared a common dream, and were only together for two years before tragedy struck. From this Higher Self perspective, tell me about David's part in this."

Judi: "David knew the part he had to play and he was prepared to play it. His love knew no end, especially for the children . . . all the children. And he was willing to go the distance and do whatever was required."

"Were the two of you together before in other lifetimes that may have set the events of this life into motion?"

Judi: "Yes. We shared great love, great adventures, fantastic journeys. I see us in a boat on a lake and he's laughing. It's a beautiful day. He's looking into my eyes and saying, 'Remember this. Never forget this day. Be happy. No problems. All is well.'"

"Where did this lifetime take place?"

Judi: "Normandy."

"What happened in this incarnation that set the current events into play?"

Trembling with emotion, Judi described a bloody battlefield in which David was killed. I wanted to explore who David might have killed prior to his own death, but Judi became so emotional, I directed her away from the scene. "No pain and no emotion . . . the emotion is just fading away. Fading away." Once she began breathing normally, I asked if she could further explain how the past was interacting with the present.

After a pause, Judi began channeling again, this time with David speaking through her: "Without my death the truth would not be known. It was necessary to bring attention to this evil. My death was a necessary part of it. I did not want you to be suffering like this, but it was inevitable. I live in your heart and in your words and in your actions. In that way I am not gone. I reside in all that you do. I am free and I am well. Do not cry for me. I love you. You and my little twins."

"Can you see David there with you, Judi? Can you feel his presence?"

Judi: "He looks like an angel. He says, 'In time, my death will help many others. I've told you this before and it is so. Trust.'"

I considered asking questions of David, but so many mediums had already done so and had received answers as to all aspects of his death and those responsible for the crime. By this time, Judi had been in trance for nearly 90 minutes, which is as long as I like to keep someone in an altered state without a break. I decided to end the session by projecting her forward into the future to explore how her dream of an orphanage would eventually manifest.

Judi: "Hawaii . . . an oasis with horses, rain forest, a white building, children on horses, laughing. I see celebrations, excitement, preparations, getting ready for visitors. People are coming. The children are excited and can't wait to show off what they've done, their garden, their greenhouse, their artwork, which is displayed in a big room. It's beautiful." She began to cry again. "There's great rejoicing for the healing of damaged children. People will come from everywhere to learn about it."

"And you're going to write about it to generate this attention?"

Judi: "Yes, plus speaking, interviews, traveling, fund raising . . . the Senate. We'll find help in many places."

Upon awakening Judi, we discussed the session. When we talked about the motive for David's murder, she said, "Some of the psychics who have helped me have also provided information about child trafficking for profit or child pornography purposes. David may have been murdered because he accidentally saw something he should not have seen regarding abducted children or drug-related activities. Solving his murder will help to uncover a larger truth relating to missing children and to public awareness of atrocities performed on children."

Currently, 700,000 children are reported missing in America every year.

Private investigator Phil Harris died of a heart attack three days after testifying in court against the nanny, regarding an incident in which she had abusively shaken a baby in her care. Judi is suspicious as to the real cause of Phil's death. She said that one of the investigators had observed the nanny in meetings with the suspected neighbor. "I've been advised that I should shut up, because my life could be in danger, but I feel protected," Judi said. "A British investigative journalist advised me to put as much information as I have into as many hands as possible. I've done that."

Today, through her Earth Harmony Foundation, Judi heads The International Children's Rights Project, which seeks to enact new legislation to protect foster children from becoming victims of illicit adoptions for trafficking and child pornography. "Social Services is only allowed to check up on children for six months after an adoption. I want that law changed," Judi said.

"David's vision for the orphanage continues. We have a house here, and we've purchased another in Hawaii. Dov and I have adopted two more special-needs children. And as more money comes into the foundation, we plan to build or buy a bigger house where the kids can have a garden, a therapy room, and other special facilities."

"How many children would you like to adopt?" Tara asked.

"Ideally, about 12. Right now, we want Tisha and Darius to be found. I believe my perseverance is the one chance they have. I've never wavered on trying to get the authorities to do something. I still make the sheets on their beds every day. I keep up their room. And I'll continue to do it, even if I never see them again, because this very act of faith allows for the possibility. And isn't that what life is all about? It's the possibility of good . . . the possibility of miracles."

To further investigate, Tara asked for Judi's astrological data plus the birth information on both David and the neighbor she has publicly accused of the murder. Tara read the birth charts and then combined them all to obtain an astrological overview.

The astrology between David and the neighbor shows a strong need for retribution and retaliation on the part of the neighbor. Something gruesome and very emotional happened between these two men in a past life. Tara had psychic flashes of several men, including David, torches in hand, burning the home of an unarmed family to punish the husband who was away fighting on the "wrong side."

Tara said, "Based upon this astrological chart, I don't believe that the neighbor will be convicted of David's murder. The karma between the two men is that David killed this man's beloved family, so therefore David died when he was most in love with his wife and family. But the chart does show that the neighbor will definitely be confined in this life—probably prison, but it could be a hospital."

When Tara completed her work on Judi's astrological chart she said, "Based upon what I can read here, I believe the two tragedies are related. On the day of David's death, she was very much in love.

But the aspect that was most intense at that time was her progressed Sun aspecting her marriage. That indicates something would shake her to the core of her being. The girdle on her Midheaven says she would lose one of the great loves of her life."

In compositing David and Judi's astrology chart, Tara found that although their aspects showed an extraordinary love for each other, there was also a tragedy. Tara said, "The chart tells me this is the last lifetime they would have to deal with this particular karma with this person." Tara also made this note on the back of the chart. "So much love, not enough time. Death aspects followed them. When one dies, the other dies in a different way."

Based upon what she saw in the chart, Tara asked for psychic impressions to help her clarify the pieces of the puzzle she was trying to assemble. This combination of astrology and psychic input resulted in the following notes: "I feel this all started with Judi being a judge at witch burnings. That comes in strong. David's past life shows good fortune and a leadership position. The American Civil War. David and the suspected murderer's composite chart says that there was a sacrifice due to fire—burning out the suspect's farm and family while the suspect was away. Judi was also involved with David in this act. In their current lives, I feel the suspect not only killed David, he helped arrange for the kids to be adopted elsewhere. Consciously or subconsciously, the suspect wanted Judi to suffer loss as he did in his past life."

In summary, Judi committed suicide in a past life because her baby was taken from her at birth. Classically, if someone commits suicide, they have to reincarnate and face a similar, but often more severe, situation without killing themselves again. This is not to punish, but to teach on a soul level that life is sacred. In this life, Judi made a soul agreement to lose her husband and have two babies taken from her. And this time around, rather than taking her life, she has channeled her energy into resolving David's murder and establishing the Earth Harmony Foundation to help all children. Out of bad often comes good, and Judi's "children's rights" efforts may save far more children than she ever could have saved through her adoptive plans. If a child pornography conspiracy is uncovered, even more children will be saved.

Obviously, David remains earthbound, obsessed with trying to resolve his murder. I am reminded of Kahlil Gibran's words in *The Prophet:* "The murdered is as guilty as the murderer." If Tara's astrological interpretation and psychic visions are correct, David made a soul contract to balance his karma with his murderer. It is now time for David to let go and embrace the light. Continued anger could keep him tied to the Earth for centuries.

Karma is a multi-life debit and credit system, and we all create our own reality, or karma, with our thoughts, words, and deeds . . . and this includes the motive, intent, and desire behind everything we think, say, and do. In other words, when we act with intent we create karma—harmonious karma or disharmonious karma—that will have to be balanced in the future.

5

Shauna, Bert, and Agnes

"Marriage and hanging go by destiny; matches are made in heaven."
                                        —Robert Burton, English writer

I was enchanted by Shauna Hoffman the moment she walked into Tara's workshop at the International Hypnosis Federation Conference. Petite, pretty, blond-haired, light-eyed, with a radiant personality, Shauna was a therapist with a practice in nearby Santa Clarita.

The three-day hypnosis conference was held on the *Queen Mary* in Long Beach, California. Those attending were hypnotists in training or professional hypnotists in practice. Shauna was there to pick up counseling credit hours. After a lengthy conversation, we exchanged e-mail addresses.

Soon after, Shauna became an e-mail buddy, whose cyber messages always made me laugh out loud. And she inspired me to write much funnier messages to her than I did to anyone else. A friendship rapidly developed. We discussed our careers, work projects, relationships, pets, and Tahiti. Shauna had been with her husband Bert for 27 years. "Did you get together when you were 12?" I asked.

"Seventeen," she said.

That made Tara and Shauna the same age—a dog year in Chinese astrology—also the birth year of Madonna, Sharon Stone, Michelle Pfeiffer, and many other intense, high-profile women. Shauna is a Leo sun, Leo moon, and Sagittarius rising. No wonder I understood and liked her. As I am an Aries with a Leo rising, it was a matter of fire relating to fire.

Shauna and Bert met in Chicago, where he owned the top jazz club. He had served in the Peace Corps in Africa and built a hospital he named "The Jimi Hendrix Children's Hospital." Today Bert is legal guardian of the cartoon character "The Rat Fink," made popular by Big Daddy Roth, the artist, car-builder icon of the 1960s. Bert is also a gardener, gourmet chef, and biologist—nicknamed "BioBert."

I did not want Shauna to think I was in contact behind Tara's back. I explained that Tara and I have many separate friends of the opposite sex, which enhances both of our lives. When one of us begins a new friendship, the individual often becomes a family friend. She wrote back: "Friends are the most important thing to me. My goal is to write a book called *Divine Friendship*. Hahahaha. My hubby has had to learn not to be jealous of me and my male friends, because I have so many. We go to lunch, movies, travel together, have deep talks, and share profound times. Sailing, hiking, whatever. They are all just souls to me. Bert and I are way past the 'ownership' stage."

One evening soon after this exchange, Tara and I met Shauna for dinner at Cha, Cha, Cha, a Caribbean restaurant in the Valley. We ended up talking for hours. Shauna revealed that she and Bert had had no children by choice. They both love island culture and decorated their home accordingly. I had told Shauna that Tara and I had reservations for a family vacation to Moorea, Tahiti, so she had brought us a bag of Tahiti travel journals and gave me money to buy Bert his favorite coconut soap.

Upon our return home from the islands, Shauna invited us to

meet her husband and attend an L.A. music showcase by one of her friends at Cafe-Club Fais Do-Do in Los Angeles. Tara and I liked Bert immediately. Shauna explained, "Bert does all the cooking. He used to stand over me and 'suggest' a lot when I cooked. So I stopped. Now I come home to shrimp or lobster, barbecue Creole, or Jamaican-style lamb. A feast every night. My friends hate me."

Shauna and I continued to develop our friendship via phone and e-mail, and provided each other with soothing advice upon hitting some "dips in the road." The more I got to know her, the more interesting she became. She had produced the first Marianne Williamson tapes on "A Course in Miracles," and she continued to produce audio/video programs for other therapists. In addition to seeing clients in therapy three days a week, she wrote, produced, and acted in a mystery "whodunit" for cruise ship passengers every other month. Shauna also took conga-drum lessons, did volunteer work for "Collie Rescue," and still managed to write regular lengthy e-mails and meet me for an occasional lunch.

She claimed to be my counselor, murder queen, acting coach, fashion consultant (in regard to Moorea), and weather girl.

Cool.

"Want to do a past-life regression?" I said. "I'd love to find out what set your current relationship with Bert into play. He'd probably like to know why he fell in love with such an independent, self-motivated woman."

Shauna was delighted by the idea and explained that her mom, Agnes, would soon be visiting from Texas. "She's an Auschwitz survivor. Might make an interesting case history for your writing about extreme circumstances."

We set a date. Bert, Shauna, and Agnes would come to our house on Sunday afternoon. Following the regression work, Tara would fix dinner.

Agnes handed me a homemade Bundt cake as she came in the front door. Shauna and I hugged and kissed. Because of an airport mix-up, Bert could not join them.

We drank wine, talked, and laughed. Agnes was a delight—possessing a variation of her daughter's captivating personality. Now in her mid-seventies, she often speaks to students in Texas schools about her Holocaust experience. Agnes was born in a small town in Hungary. Her father was a writer, so her parents were among the first taken by the Nazi invaders who targeted the Jewish intelligentsia very early on. She had three younger sisters, yet only Agnes survived the death-camp experience. The Germans evidently kept her alive because she was pretty—Aryan-looking with blue eyes and blond hair—and she could speak Hungarian and German, so was valued as a translator.

In Auschwitz, Agnes joined forces with three older girls. Blanca was closest and assumed a motherly position. They were free laborers by day in German company plants. At night they were returned to the camps, where survival often meant fighting for a potato in the soup. Toward the end of the war, Agnes and Blanca were separated and each thought the other had been killed. The day the war ended, Agnes was in a field, where she and many others were to be shot. The execution was halted by men arriving on motorcycles announcing the war was over.

Twenty years later, Agnes was walking down a Chicago street when she overheard a woman and recognized the voice. She said to the woman, "Excuse me, do I know you?"

The woman said, "I don't think so."

When Agnes heard the accent, she said, "Blanca, it's Aggie."

They broke into tears and fell into each other's arms. Since shortly after the war, they had been living ten miles apart. Agnes's family had been using Blanca's husband's dry cleaning establishment for years.

I would call that a fated meeting. I could have asked Agnes questions for hours, but it was time to do some past-life regression work. Shauna volunteered to go first.

Tara agreed to psychically monitor Shauna's regression, so once the body relaxation was complete, I directed a chakra link between the two women, who imagined their crown, brow, and throat energy centers connected by bands of colored light. Following the countdown, I said, "We're going to move way, way back in time, Shauna. We'll begin by looking at your relationship with Bert. What brought the two of you together, if indeed something happened in another time and another place that set this union into play? The two of you may have been together many times, but let's look at what established the conditions of your current life. If you have not been with Bert in the past, then you will explore the situations that formed the relationship you share today. As the impressions form, I'd like you to speak up and tell me what you perceive . . . what you are doing?"

"I see a river . . . I'm standing on a rock on the edge of the river, just watching the water flow by." We established that she was alone, a female, barefooted, in her middle teens, wearing a "peasanty" kind of dress. "I'm very happy-go-lucky, just watching the river. This is my domain . . . my place."

I moved her forward in time. She said, "I sense a very mean man. Very dark feeling. He's my father. Screaming at me. He wants to know where I've been. Why am I always so frivolous? I should be doing something . . . working on the farm . . . cooking." (Shauna snickered at the idea of cooking.)

"Do you have any brothers or sisters?" I asked.

"No brothers or sisters, no mother. I'm the daughter, and I'm supposed to be the son, the wife, the daughter."

I asked her to describe her surroundings and she said the house was "sparse and small." She was living in Alabama in 1882. In regard to her relationship with her father: "It's not even abuse, it's just expectations. He's an angry man." When I asked how she responded to him, she said, "I'm not compliant. I go to the river."

"What goes through your mind while you're at the river? Do you dream of . . ."

"Bigger things. Being away from there."

I directed her to move forward until something important happened.

"I'm in my late twenties, dressed very nicely . . . and I'm fighting for woman's rights. I'm trying to empower women. I see a dress, a skirt and a top, and my hair up . . . and a hat and a parasol. And I'm proud I'm not that little girl on the farm."

We establish that she is part of an organization supporting this cause. "A very political organization," she said. "I don't see this, I sense it. I see me, but I can sense the work I'm supposed to do."

"Let's move forward in time to explore how far you take this work."

"I'm settled. San Francisco. But I'm alone."

She was 35 and admitted that she had been unwilling to accept a relationship when she had an opportunity, because she had chosen independence. "I work, typing, I write. I'm a writer. But I'm lonely," she said.

Her work was published in a newspaper column about women's rights. I asked her how the people of San Francisco reacted to her views. "The women and the nouveau-riche men love it. It's a fad to them, but I believe in it."

She sometimes spoke at rallies. "I led them when I was younger. Now I just speak at them."

I directed her to look at the most important people in her life. "My editor," she said quickly. "He feels like Bert. He believes in the cause. He believes in me. He supports me, but he's just my friend. Maybe he wants more, but I don't know how to give it. It would mean I need him."

"And you fear this?"

"It would prove me wrong."

I asked questions about her relationship with her editor. "I trust him," she said. "I can rely on him. He's always there for me."

Upon moving her forward in time to an important situation, she said, "I'm in a hospital. I have no energy." She was 38 to 40 years old. "I'm going to die. Very pale. I don't really care since I've done what I needed to do. I'm peaceful and free. He visits me. He's by my bed, crying. I smile at him and say, 'It's okay.'"

When Shauna was projected forward into spirit, shortly after leaving her physical body, she said, "My father is there. My mother. And I have a little lamb that's there."

"How do you feel about seeing your father?"

"He's smiling. But I feel distant."

She observed the physical body she had just left. I asked for her response to experiencing this transition. She said, "Relief . . . ready . . . calm."

"Do you feel you accomplished what you set out to do in the lifetime?" I asked.

"I feel some sadness over having experienced no love. But proud."

I counted Shauna back into the present before directing her up into Higher Self. We called in her spirit guides and Master teachers. "Now you saw the man you assumed to be Bert in the lifetime we just explored. Can you provide me with a karmic overview of your past relationships with Bert?"

"There was also a time that he was my brother. And there was something in the army. They thought I was a young boy, but I was a girl. Fighting. I see my hair cut short. Wearing a helmet. Trying to pretend I am male . . . and he was there."

"When was this?"

"Sixteen hundreds in England. I want to fight." We established that Bert was her superior officer in the conflicts. "He was calm, and I was feisty. I wanted to fight. They killed my family."

Next I directed her to explore any past-life relationships she had experienced with her present-day mother, Agnes.

"I see that we feel like we're sisters . . . best friends. Holding hands and skipping. The countryside. Playing. We're avoiding the war. There's a war and we're pretending it is not happening. Playing with rocks on the hillside. She has blue eyes and pigtails. We're laughing. Making bonds like we're sisters. But I think we're really afraid of the armies that are coming."

Upon my moving her ahead in time, she said, "They're burning houses, and we're running to our houses. And I don't see her anymore. We're trying to find our families. The houses are burning and the people are running and screaming. There are men on horses and they're laughing. I go to my home, and it's burned. It's gone. I can't find my parents."

I moved her out of this traumatic situation and forward in time. She then saw herself sitting in a classroom. "They're telling me to study. I'll need to learn."

"What has happened between the time your house was burned and right now?"

"A family took me and brought me to another village. I'm supposed to stay there and go to school."

"What about your friend?"

"I don't know where she is."

When I attempted to move her forward in time to further

explore this incarnation, she said, "I can't see anything." I assumed this was to avoid pain, so I called in her spirit guides to have them tell her what happened.

Shauna spoke haltingly, as if repeating the words she was hearing. "A family is not just blood. It's who you trust and who you love and who is there for you. And it goes on forever. You can feel them forever, still with you. Even if you don't see them anymore. I could feel her presence. Always."

Upon awakening Shauna, we all discussed the regression. Tara had been drawing impressions through the chakra link and writing them down. She had picked up vivid images of Shauna as a women's rights advocate, and she also wrote, "In many lifetimes she has been without a man and has had to raise children alone: Africa, New Guinea, Peru, Spain, Maracabo. She has had several island lifetimes but ended up feeling very lonely. Starving situations with children. Being panicked. Life can be cruel—too cruel for people she loves. She decides against bringing more children into this unrestful world."

In a Sioux Indian incarnation, "She is very much in love. Her husband is taken from her, killed by white army men. She is mourning for him—wailing for his soul. She has three children from him. There is war with the army. They all die. Most of the tribe dies. A few escape to the Northland.

"Shauna is tied to the Earth. Loves Earth-style religions, as well as Paganism, Zen, native-type worship. She tries to understand a higher form of ceremony but sees the problems created by men in power. She has been a pope, poisoned when too involved with a Spanish king.

"Blue dress, very pretty, high society. Bert is a soldier. They are at a dance. He is going to Africa as an escort to diplomats. He asks her to marry him as he courts her for six weeks while supplies are prepared. He leaves, never returns. She longs for him the rest of her life."

Tara also perceived powerful images of Shauna dying in a German gas chamber at the age of 12 or 13. "She was someone who was close to her current mother."

Both Tara and Shauna said they felt Shauna was one of Agnes's sisters who had died in a German death camp.

Hypnotizing Agnes, I directed her to go back to a lifetime that established her need to experience Auschwitz. But after a 50-minute session in which we perceived little information, I assumed she was subconsciously blocking. When memories are very painful, this is sometimes the case.

As Shauna had mentioned in an e-mail a week earlier, "I think that to survive, Mom went into a very healthy denial of her Auschwitz experience."

Rather than further pursue this horrific chain of cause and effect, we all ate dinner, drank more wine, and enjoyed Agnes's fabulous Bundt cake.

A few days after the regression, Shauna did some Web research to see if a pope had ever been poisoned for his association with a Spanish king, as Tara had perceived. Many popes were involved with Spanish kings and not all their deaths can be explained. But in 1517, adversaries led by Cardinal Petrucci attempted to poison Pope Leo X, who was connected to the Spanish king.

Although not religious today, Shauna is very spiritual. While e-mail corresponding about the right and wrong of the 2003 Iraq war, she wrote, ". . . the choice is a spiritual one. I do not have the right to kill. Even if they want to kill me first. I am just spirit in bodily form. What I do to keep this body should not go against spirit. Too much karma to pay. So they can kill me. I will go on to something better. They won't."

To further investigate this case history, Tara examined Shauna's astrological chart and a composite chart with her husband, Bert. My wife prepared an astrology wheel and made hundreds of tiny notes on the page. She then read three esoteric astrological systems in combination to arrive at her conclusions. I have been around a lot of astrologers, but I've never seen anyone else approach a reading in this way. I have also never seen anyone as accurate. Here is what Tara had to say about Shauna and Bert, based only upon the mathematics of the charts.

In Shauna's individual chart, she had a fated meeting with Bert on the soul goal aspect. She really wanted to marry Bert in this life, but he would not have been emotionally sure about this at first. Physically there was never a choice. The past life most affecting Shauna is probably one full of accomplishment and social standing—a fortunate past life.

Looking at their combined chart, there was an important shared incarnation in which Shauna and Bert had a big life, in high society or in government. There was a sudden parting— karma in the parting, because Bert died.

In this life, Pluto, the planet that forces transformation, is the jet fuel in their lives. They *were* going to be married, no way around it. They have a lot of luck. There are intense indicators of luck, treasure, profit, praise, speculation. The Sun at 13 degrees is very important to this union. Seven degrees Scorpio rising and their Moon is at 14 degrees Scorpio. Their sex drive sits on their Sun. Sudden luck sits on their Sun. These two were truly born again to be together. They are soulmates.

But even though they're soulmates, there is needed learning. They have had to learn to work around each other's temperament. Their emotions sit in the first house (the house of personality and how you relate to life and present yourself to the world), so they're right up front with emotions. They can get emotional and frustrated with each other—rigid and opinionated. There is karma to be wrestled with. When it comes to their freedom, they hold something over each other resulting in some kind of subtle emotional restrictions. But there is benevolence that comes in to save them here . . . emotionally it all works out in the wash.

They have had to scramble at different times to make ends meet financially, but they adjust fast to change, and all in all, they should be well provided for when they allow each other to achieve individual business goals. Change has come with luck again to save them. Not to say that a combination business wouldn't serve them well, but they would have to be emotionally adjustable and fair with each other.

They share a belief in higher order and ideals. They have very strong opinions about the world and are rarely superficially motivated in conversation. Bert and Shauna each believe in the other's integrity and ideas on a very deep level.

Meeting each other occurred under unusual circumstances, but upon meeting there would be no turning back, because the astrological aspects are *way* too powerful. In the area of career, there have been some disappointments, but there is always hope and faith in each other. These two are not necessarily perceived as a typical couple. They are seen as unusual, even in regard to their careers and interests.

They do have a hard time catching up to each other occasionally. There is lots of energy, but it doesn't always go in the same direction. Another one of their karmic tests relates to the unusual freedom aspects reflected here. They sometimes feel like they are not getting enough together time—love time. Meddling relatives or friends are not tolerated for long, because there are astrological factors here to quell this.

Unusual is the theme in their marriage. They don't want to conform to what is known as "traditional marriage," but they do have traditional love for each other. They are under each other's skin and always will be.

When Tara finished the above astrological reading, I sent it as an e-mail to Shauna and asked, "How accurate is this?" The following is what I received in return:

"Okay, this was perfect! We both read it together and agree it is right on. The line about being rigid and opinionated . . . we both laughed and tried to blame the other one. Okay we *both are!* We both respect and demand our independence—have from the beginning, so the chart is right on there, too. I could go on and on. Actually there is nothing that felt like it didn't fit for us. Pretty wild. We both gave each other big kisses and smiled knowing we were meant to be together. Thank you both. This was great for us, for our Saturday together! Love ya, Shauna."

At the bottom of all Shauna e-mails appears this line after her signature: "Remember . . . Miracles shall follow miracles and wonders shall never cease!"

In summary: Shauna's current life is a natural extension of her most recent past lives. She campaigned for women's rights in the past, and she is living the life of a married but liberated woman in the present. It is wise to keep in mind, when we vote and support causes, we are creating the world we will one day reincarnate back into.

Shauna was a writer in San Francisco, and today she writes "whodunit" mysteries, conducts seminars, and is planning to write a self-help book on relationships. By choosing not to have children, Shauna and Bert could focus their energy upon each other—something they had not been able to do for many lifetimes. And, as Tara pointed out, there was a decision, based upon past-life pain, not to bring more children into "this unrestful world." The fact that she died in a World War II concentration camp reinforces her antiwar/pro-peace beliefs today.

6

Meghan Hansen

"Whatever may befall thee, it was preordained for thee from everlasting."
—Marcus Aurelius Antoninus

I arrived at Meghan Hansen's Universal Records office a half hour late due to rush-hour Beverly Hills traffic. We were to meet for a leisurely dinner, then catch Matt Nathanson's set at the Troubadour—the world-famous West Hollywood rock club. Meghan had discovered Matt, a rocker/singer songwriter, had signed him to the label, and was currently managing the production of his first album.

Meghan's assistant, Aimee, met me in the empty penthouse lobby and guided me to the inner sanctum. Meghan and I hugged and said our hellos, and I teased the two women about being the only workaholics in the company. It was 7:00 P.M. The huge office appeared empty.

Aimee nodded . . . rolling her eyes. Meghan laughed. She is

young, beautiful, and tall with long brown hair to her waist. Upon first meeting her, you sense a shyness. Upon getting to know her, you wonder why you ever thought that.

I have known Meghan since she attended one of my seminars years ago. The past few years we have been in closer contact, exchanging e-mails a couple times a week. Tara and I invite her to parties and family gatherings at our house. She invites us to show-cases and club events. We share a love of metaphysics and a passion for hiking. On our last shared hiking adventure, Meghan and I climbed up to Native American cliff-side dwellings hidden in an Arizona canyon.

To maintain her position in the company, Meghan has been working a double shift since the label downsized due to faltering fortunes in the music industry. She and Aimee seldom leave the office before nine, when Meghan is expected to check out new artists appearing in the hottest clubs. If someone with potential appears, Universal wants an opportunity to sign them before Columbia, Virgin, or Sony can. She usually ends her work day around midnight.

Universal Music Group, the parent company, is actually comprised of about 80 record labels and maintains 30 percent of the music market worldwide. Meghan just finished working on Edie Brickell's new album and is in the process of gathering information for label copy and credits.

I was sitting on an overstuffed white couch lining one wall of her office. "How many albums are you currently producing?"

Meghan handed me a half-frozen bottle of water and counting on her fingers, said, "Seven albums."

The view from the penthouse was spectacular. Downtown Los Angeles appeared hazy in the distance. Electronics and a state-of-the-art sound system filled a good portion of the office. Stacks of promotional CDs lined shelving beneath the huge window wall. Recording project files lined the space on the floor between the speakers. I asked a question about the sales of a particular album. She punched up a Sound Scan report on her computer and shared the numbers.

When we get together, I enjoy talking music with this lady. She explained how she had recently managed a licensing project and gave millions of Universal's dollars in royalty money to songwriters and publishing companies that had not known to claim the bounty. She was assigned to find out who was owed what and see that the money was fairly distributed.

Educated at the State University of New York, Meghan received her degree in classical music. Her work history included a stint in the promotional department of *Guitar* magazine, then on to the promotion department of Geffen Records, followed by a position as marketing manager for Sony Music in New York. She returned to Los Angeles to take a position with Sony and was soon promoted to A&R (artist and repertoire). Columbia Records followed, then Universal, with the A&R title and all the responsibilities that accompanied it.

The way she handled her executive duties was fascinating enough, but her highly tuned intuition added to the intrigue. She was very psychic, sometimes to her detriment.

Over dinner in a nearby deli, she told me that five years ago she had had a vision in which she would discover a talented new artist at the Troubadour, where she first saw Matt Nathanson. "His demo CD wasn't too amazing, but when I saw him perform live, I knew he was a star."

I wondered how much of this was intuition and how much could be credited to her natural feel for the contemporary music market. She had good reason to hope Matt would become a star, considering she has a point in his recording deal. She also had put herself on the line, because she should only sign people she believed could sell a minimum of a half-million albums—something very difficult for a new artist to do. Anything less and the label would drop the artist.

"Tara, Hunter, and Cheyenne all asked me to thank you for the latest Universal care package," I said. The previous week she had sent a large box of vinyls (disco and techno) for my teenage son and daughter, both of whom are learning to "spin" on dual turntables. Tara quickly ran off with most of the new rock CDs.

Our conversation soon drifted to remote viewing—the psychic spying technique used by the U.S. government in "Project Stargate."

She had sent me a copy of a book she had just read. I shared some interesting case histories she was not aware of.

At nine that evening, we made our way through the standing-room-only crowd at the Troubadour. A mediocre duo played on stage. "What do you think?" she shouted in my ear. I gave her a thumbs down. She nodded in agreement, and we made our way back out to an adjoining bar where we could talk over a drink.

"Island Records just signed them," she said, shaking her head.

A female friend of Meghan's from Sony Soundtrax joined us in the bar. We talked until Matt took the stage.

I recognized what had so impressed Meghan. Not only does Matt Nathanson have a unique voice, he exhibits a seasoned stage presence and a delightful, self-effacing personality. He charmed and teased the edgy West Hollywood audience, many of whom were mouthing the lyrics to his songs. Obviously, he appeared here regularly. Halfway through a 90-minute set, he cajoled the audience into participating in a classic audience-bonding singalong. It was over-the-top and tongue-in-cheek, but to my surprise everyone played the game.

After the set, Meghan and I joined Matt backstage. He was 30 years old, wrote his own songs, had been on the road for ten years, and he had not slept in three days because he was participating in the mixing of his new album. I liked his music, and I liked him.

"You did good by signing him," I told Meghan as we hugged goodnight.

Meghan's life revolves around music. She does her job by the book, but I believe she also channels considerable psychic energy into all aspects of her life. For some people the veil between this world and the spirit world is thin. Those on the Other Side can more easily influence some people, even physically influence them. Three weeks earlier, Meghan had sent me an excited e-mail. "All meaningful things happen for me on the second and twenty-second of the month," she said. "All day Friday, I felt like someone or something was trying to speak to me. I was out of it all day. My emotions were on overload. I really wanted to go home and get to my keyboard, to work on a song I felt was ready to come through me. But by the time I was leaving the office, I was dizzy and it was pouring rain. I didn't want to drive all the way home to the Palisades, so I decided to check out one of the local clubs. I was told by spirit to go to the Viper Room, which I did.

"The band and singer were awesome. I never get this lucky (hence I only sign two or three artists/bands a year). The place was packed wall to wall, and the reaction this kid got from the crowd was just amazing. The next day, when I told my boss I wanted to sign them, she asked me if I thought this was a band Bob Ezrin could work with. Halfway into my conversation with the band manager, he asked me, 'If we sign, would you mind if Bob Ezrin produces the album?'"

"So spirit manipulated you to the Viper Room?" I wrote.

"It's possible."

But there is also a darker side to Meghan's spiritual connections. On March 2, 1996, she felt compelled to call Keri, her younger sister, who lived in New York City. There was no answer. Meghan began to have mental flashes of her mother's anger killing her sister. The room began to whirl, and she fainted. At that moment, her sister had killed herself more than 3,000 miles away. The phone call, verified by records, was at the exact time of her sister's death.

I decided Meghan might make an interesting case history for this book. She agreed to explore past-life regression at our home on a Saturday afternoon. Prior to the session, we talked about what she wanted to find out. She said she was interested in why she is so intuitive and why others have so often taken credit for what she does. When perceiving an important vision, she often faints in response. Upon meeting a man in the music industry in New York, she saw herself marrying him. She knew they had been musical composers who had shared a past life. Thoughts swirled through her mind. "He put his name on some music I composed. I'll marry him in this life, and this time I'll get credit." And she almost fainted but caught herself before passing out.

"I'd like to know about the relationship between us," Meghan said. "After meeting him, I knew nothing would happen for a while. He was married. But I knew I'd meet him again three years later in California. I even perceived who would bring us together. It happened as in the vision. He is now in the process of divorce."

Meghan made herself comfortable on the couch. Once she was

hypnotized, I instructed her to go back to the beginning of her manifestations of psychic ability. She soon began describing a mountainous vista. "But no one has bodies," she said. After extensive questioning, I found she was a spiritual being who communicated with others mind to mind. In time, there would be a soul-crossover—a period when nonphysical beings would begin to explore the potentials of physical bodies by inhabiting the Earth.

I smiled upon realizing she had literally returned to the very beginning of her intuitive communications, just as I had directed.

I moved Meghan up into Higher Self, explaining that from this level she would have knowledge of her soul history, and we could quickly obtain considerable information.

"We just completed exploring a time when you were in spirit as light and awareness. Since then, I assume you've experienced many Earth incarnations."

Meghan: "Hundreds."

"Let's begin by exploring your nearly fainting upon meeting your friend in the music business. Why did this happen?"

Meghan: "We've been together forever. Neither of us can fulfill our mission on Earth without the other. Love and work . . . but always to help others."

"Can you tell me what will happen between the two of you in the future?"

Meghan: "We're going to write a song that will help people understand that war isn't real. People will understand through a song, not a newspaper. We're not together yet, but it has to be soon. The whole world needs the song. Our spirit guides will help us fulfill the mission, but since we have free will, we have not yet combined our energy."

She took a deep breath, paused, then said, "The spirits tell me things. The week before September 11, 2001, I perceived the Tarot Tower card and the Devil, but I didn't pay any further attention. If I had stopped, I would have seen the full vision. That's why when they want me to listen, they make me faint."

"This was the situation when your sister died in New York?"

Meghan: "My sister died because I killed myself in my last life in 1911. Germany."

"Can you explain this?"

Meghan: "I killed myself. She was devastated by my death. But she came back and she died this time to show me what I put her through and how wrong it was."

"Why did you take your life?"

Meghan: "I was female. My sister was named Maria. In that life my father was very violent, and it was just miserable to live there. I was nine years old and I couldn't stand it anymore, so I died. I took my life by hanging."

"And in this life it was your mother who was violent?"

Meghan: "Yes."

"Is the karma between you and your sister balanced now?"

Meghan: "It is balanced. When I get married, she'll be my first daughter."

"All right, I'd like to explore the situation of other people taking credit for what you do. You say in another time and place, your friend stole music you wrote?"

Meghan: "I would not have been prepared for this incarnation without that one. People have taken credit for what I do in this life, but I'm going through this because we are all learning a lesson. They need to realize that it's important to be a part of something. But everyone knows who does the work. They'll fall for taking credit. I'm learning that credit isn't the most important thing. In the past-life situation it should not have meant so much to me."

"Because you were so upset in the past life, you returned in a somewhat similar situation to learn to rise above such feelings? To be tested again?"

Meghan: "Yes."

"You're in a glamorous business, and you're very successful at a young age. You produce music that is heard by millions of people. Can you talk to me about the karma that set this into play?"

Meghan: "I've had many lifetimes all about music. In this life, I needed to see how people can touch others, the public, because I would not be able to do it myself without seeing how it is done by others. So I make records and people hear them . . . and the artists I work with are publicly known. And I am to learn from them about being present with such a large audience. And that's why I work for a record company. I will, however, change back to an artist in the future. This is to show me, because I was very shy in this life. My spirits say I withhold gifts I could use to help others."

Upon awakening Meghan, we discussed her experience. Tara joined us and asked for Meghan's astrological data, so she could add this dimension of understanding to what we already knew.

Meghan is a Leo Sun with a Capricorn Moon and Gemini Rising. Tara began the reading, saying:

> I see a prominent past life in which Meghan loved her mother, who had her out of wedlock and under bad circumstances. The mother was a maid to a European nobleman. Meghan inherited many opportunities because her father took care of her. But in time, she became involved with witches, and although she helped many others, when she was in need, her father died. I saw death by fire. Through that experience, she values her father very much in this life, and she lacks trust in others, in general.
>
> In this life, she is very ambitious and uses her intuition, which sits on Rigel, a Persian royal star. So even her bad luck usually ends up serving her. Her fascination is with her money and stability . . . and she is reorienting herself, always. Life isn't always as fun as she would like it to be, but there is a great deal of power and protection around these aspects.
>
> In her love life, the right partnership will only be with someone whom she connects with mentally as well as physically. He will have to be magical, mysterious, and deep thinking. Meghan's intelligence is reflected here, along with divine guidance, and her love of learning and talking. Learning brings her emotional peace.
>
> In her career, she needs to be able to shine in her own atmosphere to do her best. Pluto sits in Leo, trined with Libra, so this jet fuel drives her forward in a good but odd way. She brings unusual work into her life and could be successful in her own career as easily as she is in working for corporations. Public honor, happiness, and friends . . . she sometimes feels like friends don't fulfill her. It feels as if she isn't sure of their

motives, yet the friends she does have can bring her great happiness. I see karma in the area of romance. She is in good aspect to romance, but love will have to meet her standards for the energy to manifest.

She has considerable good luck in the area of service to others. Meghan is going to transform a few times with her careers, but it should bring her money and every time she does, she should use her intuition to go forward again, because she has a lot of luck here. Strong interest in the occult, psychology, and mysteries is indicated and brings her great joy. Keen perception. She really strives to be her own woman. I see exile and radical adjustment in the chart, which may be her moving from New York to come to Los Angeles. Los Angeles feels good for her.

She is driven to succeed. She has hope and association with others, mother love and marriage, which often means coming together with people you already have karma with—good karma and soul contracts. She has influence. Her energy goes up and down a bit, but if she stays with it, she'll find the energy to move forward into the future, and there is a lot of luck associated with career.

Her most intense aspects are treasure and profit, so she will make it big in this life. Social standing and cooperation and contracts are indicated here as well. It is her Dharma to lead others into success as well.

In summary: Meghan's astrological chart mirrors her life, and her hypnotic explorations offer valuable karmic lessons. She has incarnated again into a life centered upon music. When we are obsessed with something—art, music, soldiering, horses, mountain climbing, seafaring, etc.—we are likely to reincarnate to experience further involvement with the subject that is so important to us. As an added dimension to her musical karma, Meghan was upset in a past life when her lover took credit for music she had written. This resentment needed to be resolved, so she incarnated into a musical life, and she has again experienced others taking credit for her accomplishments. Hopefully, this time, she will pass her test by rising above the resentment.

If Meghan marries the past-life lover who took credit for her work, I assume relationship tests will follow in an attempt to balance the karma between the two of them. The fact that she has already been tested in this area in her work may have mitigated the karma, making it easier to deal with this breach of faith on an even more personal level.

In a past life, Meghan took her own life, leaving her sister devastated. This time around, her sister Keri took her life to provide Meghan with a lesson. Although that will sound like a stretch to most readers, I have encountered similar situations with other people. Keep in mind the bigger picture. For reasons that may be far deeper than just to provide Meghan with a lesson, Keri made a decision to do what she did. Everyone in the family and all her friends were affected, so it was their karma as well, and there is no way to know how all the puzzle pieces fit together.

As I finalized this manuscript, Meghan was also establishing her own A&R consulting company—Purple Dolphin Music. Some popular singers had commissioned her to help find songs for upcoming albums, and an organization had offered her the opportunity to start a new record label. Whatever directions she decides to follow in the future, I believe she will be very successful.

7

Katherine Brooks

"I am the mistress of my fate."
                    —William Shakespeare

Upon meeting Katherine Brooks, age 26, Tara and I were fascinated by this beautiful, dark-haired young woman. Katherine was intense, brooding, and serious, but always ready with big smile and a laugh that sounded like she was responding to an inside joke.

"What do you do?" I asked.

"I'm a writer, actor, and a director," she said.

You don't say things like that in Los Angeles. These are code words for "waitress," "dreamer," and "flake." In Katherine's case, however, the truth went even further. At the time, she was working as a freelance camera operator on various cable and network shows. She had also written, acted, directed, and managed to finance a short film. Upon seeing her work, to say that I was impressed was an understatement.

Tara and Katherine became friends, with Katherine joining a

group that gathered at our house every full moon to do "sourcing" in the backyard. Soon, Tara and Katherine were the primary partners at this monthly ritual. Not only did they respect each other's demonstrable psychic abilities, they learned that by combining their energy, they could manifest results.

At the first session that Katherine attended, after a meditative period, Tara turned to her and said, "I saw your spirit guide. He's an androgynous male who looks just like you. He climbed on a beautiful painted elephant surrounded by devotees."

"Oh, you *did* see him," Katherine said. She went on to explain that her guide was named Babaji, an East Indian immortal, who always appeared to be in his mid-twenties.

When Tara shared this with me, the name Babaji didn't mean anything. I was familiar with gurus such as Sai Baba and Osho. I quoted Osho often. But to the best of my knowledge, Babaji had never entered my consciousness. When Tara showed me his picture in a book, I agreed that he could have been a male version of Katherine dressed in East Indian attire.

I did not participate in the full-moon events, so I asked Tara to explain what they did. "We pull down the energy of the Universe and use the moon as the spotlight to focus desire. We use the moon in a positive way, visualizing the energy that will generate the right people and the right opportunities to manifest in our lives. The idea is to open the karma and release the blocks that are keeping you from having what you want. You don't always get what you want. You get what you need. Growing can be a painful process. If you want something, you may have to give up something to get it. But we all need to stay focused on our paths.

"Katherine was anxious to push her career forward, so I asked her, 'What do you most desire—to act, to write, or to direct?' She said she wanted to direct, so that's what we focused upon manifesting. As a result, Katherine has had to experience a lot of changes, some of them painful."

"And you helped to guide her to manifest opportunities to direct?" I said.

"I helped guide her into bringing her energy into alignment, so she could become clear on her intent. We guide each other in this way. We can do this for 20 minutes, or sometimes we're lying on a blanket looking up at the moon for three or four hours, depending upon how warm it is outside. We hold hands and experiment with occult techniques, often making future predictions for each other. If one of us perceives the presence of someone in spirit offering advice or a prediction, we verbalize it."

Within months of their initial sourcing, Katherine wrote and directed a short film titled *Dear Emily,* which was to be one of several shorts in a film to air on a major cable network. We attended a showing at the Director's Guild in Hollywood, enjoyed the film, and were extremely proud of Katherine.

At this time, Katherine was a camera operator on *The Osbournes*—a top-rated cable show on MTV. Upon seeing her short film, MTV offered her the opportunity to become director of the show. She accepted and her career began to take off.

On Saturday, March 15, 2003, Tara threw a twenty-seventh birthday party for Katherine at our house. Katherine came early to help Tara with the preparations. During a quiet period well before the party was to begin, I asked her if she was willing to do the hypnosis work we had talked about for so long. She agreed.

Prior to the session, I asked Katherine what she wanted to explore. She explained that two years ago, Babaji just came into her life, and she was interested in the connection to him. She also wanted to know, "Is film directing my true calling, as opposed to acting, which I love to do . . . and writing?"

"What about your adoption?" I asked, knowing this was a big issue in her life. "Tell me about that."

"My birth mother was very young and had to give me up. I was adopted when I was four days old. My life growing up was awful . . . physical, sexual, and emotional abuse."

I asked Katherine if we should have Babaji help us obtain the answers, if he was willing. She liked the idea, so I had her lie back on the couch in our living room and begin to breathe deeply. Tara was there to monitor. Since Katherine was a well-conditioned subject, I directed a body relaxation and a countdown and then moved her quickly into Higher Self and said, "I would like you to call out and ask Babaji to come in and be with you now, if he is willing to communicate through you."

After a lengthy pause, Katherine said, "He wants to know if you want to talk to me or you want to talk to him."

"Well, let's talk to him first. He may be able to answer some of the questions more directly. Babaji, why have you chosen to come through Katherine?"

Katherine hesitated and her breathing was labored until Babaji began to speak through her in an East Indian accent. As she talked, she began to spin her hands in a strange manner. "She is a chosen disciple. I have promised to always be in a physical body for the people I teach. It is difficult to speak through this particular instrument because she is strong willed and fights very hard. It is sometimes difficult to communicate."

"But she is cooperative," I said. "She wants your wisdom to come through. Why is she a chosen disciple?"

Katherine/Babaji: "She chose."

"Prior to being born in this life, she chose?" I asked.

Katherine/Babaji: "In every life, she has chosen. But I feel that in this life there is an ego of wanting too much power. That is what we are trying to break."

"Yet she would like to be very good at what she does. Is this wrong?" I said.

Katherine/Babaji: "Nothing is wrong. Just what suits her. And it is a struggle—a duality—she fights with herself. The path that has been chosen for her and the path that she is choosing are a paradox she tries to figure out. But she will never understand and must just let go."

"Can you elaborate a little more on the path she chose prior to birth? The path you would ideally like to see her walking," I said.

Katherine/Babaji: "I would ideally like to see her walking the path of the messenger and channeling, but she . . ."

I interrupted, "Communicating spiritual messages to many people?"

Katherine/Babaji: "Very, very, very, very many people."

"Don't you feel she can communicate these message through her work in film? The more power she attains, the more she will be able to communicate with a mass audience."

Katherine/Babaji: "This is correct, but she seems to be allured by the riches and glamour, and not what her work is really about. That is why I always try to come through and communicate with her—to keep her focused on the bigger picture."

"Does she have a history of Hindu lifetimes?"

Katherine/Babaji: "All."

"All? Approximately how many incarnations would that be?"

Katherine/Babaji: "Approximately five thousand."

"Yet Katherine chose to be reborn in America this time. Why break the pattern?" I said.

Katherine/Babaji: "Change. Teaching. Change and teaching."

"So the awareness of the Hindu lifetimes would come to fruition, to share them with a wider audience?"

Katherine/Babaji: "Yes. Using mass media. It would be difficult for a yogi to come and make movies." Katherine/Babaji giggled, causing me to laugh as well.

"I understand. If Katherine were only channeling and doing spiritual work, she could not make the movies. She has to make a choice. Do you, Babaji, think this a wrong choice she is making?"

Katherine/Babaji: "The choice is the same path. She is losing touch with the reasoning why this path is hers and why she chose to reincarnate into this being."

It seemed to me that Babaji was nit-picking, so I asked, "Would you communicate with her now, in the clearest language, where you feel she is making a mistake? I realize there are no mistakes from a karmic perspective, but as someone concerned with Katherine making the maximum amount of progress in this life, what advice can you offer to bring her into balance . . . and to fulfill her Dharma?"

Katherine/Babaji: "Let go of all personal dramas. Only focus upon the path, and the work and the purpose."

"Has Katherine usually devoted her lives to a spiritual quest or has she worked at different occupations?"

Katherine/Babaji: "Purely spiritual."

"I feel that Katherine has a great deal of natural writing and directing talent that may have come from prerequisite lifetimes."

Katherine (she answers in first person, for the first time since the beginning of the session): "There is this cave—a place where I have been for a very, very long time. The cave has been my creative palette. Here, I focused my imagination, but I needed to come to America to actualize my creativity. I needed to express it."

"So you changed the circumstances—not only nationality, but gender, and your approach to spirituality."

Katherine: "I wanted maximum evolutionary change."

"Why were you, Katherine, adopted into a family where you experienced considerable abuse? Why did you have to go through something like that?"

Katherine: "Because I wanted the exact opposite of everything I had previously experienced."

"Feeling that you were spiritually ready for this?"

Katherine: "Yes. This is hard to put into words, but this was a noble test—to experience the polar opposite of everything you have ever experienced. And then overcoming that to return to the place where you first started."

"Tempering the steel. Okay." I noticed a shift in Katherine's demeanor and sensed Babaji had stepped back in. "If Katherine would be more open to the channeling with you, Babaji, would she still be able to pursue a career in writing, directing, and acting?"

Katherine/Babaji: "Yes. Even more. The fame that she desires . . . if she would just let go and see the bigger picture, it would be happening like that."

"If she would just let go, envision what she desires . . ."

Katherine/Babaji: "And remember the cave. And she'll know that."

"Katherine is very good at three different things: writing, directing, acting. They seem to go hand in hand," I said. "But to fulfill her Dharma, would it be better if she were to focus all of her attention upon just one particular area?"

Katherine/Babaji: "The three areas are symbolic representations of father, mother, and child. The actor being the child, the director being the father, and the writer being the mother. Katherine wants to experience all three of these in one lifetime, so she will do all three."

"Then you would not direct her to focus more upon one than the other?"

Katherine/Babaji: "Correct."

"Okay. Katherine is here with karma to resolve, Dharma to fulfill. What is the best possible direction she could take at this time?"

There is a long pause before Katherine speaks in first person.

Katherine: "This is so crazy. I can see Babaji sitting right across from me. And there is this . . . I can't describe it. It is like he is opening his mouth and speaking, but I can't hear anything. I really feel like he wants me to make movies that teach spiritual awareness. But he says that it is becoming like a fad . . . that it has to be . . . I have to be very careful . . . to choose my words carefully in regard to what I want to express. The word 'spirituality' is becoming very faddy. Like, 'Oh, I'm a spiritual person.' So Babaji is telling me that I need to be very careful, but I do need to communicate this through my work."

"Babaji, is there anything else you would like to say to Katherine?"

Babaji: "This year is going to be an amazing year. This is a year of transition. There will be two huge projects. There will be major connections with important people. They will open a lot of doors."

"I want you to move forward in time. Further into the future. What is coming?"

Babaji: "Much fame, considerable travel, you will affect the lives of many, a lot of charities. Education."

After thanking Babaji for participating with us in this session, I awakened Katherine with positive suggestions. We both decided there would be value in further sessions with Babaji. But for the moment, it was time to celebrate Katherine's birthday.

The above hypnosis session took place on Saturday. On Sunday, Tara and I didn't get up until noon. We like to read the *Los Angeles Times* and do card readings in bed. I decided I was going to read during the afternoon. We have thousands of books on the shelves in our home because we buy them and many publishers send them to us for review or in hopes we will offer them for sale in *Soaring Spirit* magazine.

I walked around the house and pulled out several titles I was not familiar with, in hopes of finding some inspiration for my weekly Web column. I took the books upstairs and lay back in the comfy couch in the TV room. The first book I picked up was *Nothing in This*

Book Is True, but That's Exactly How Things Are. Tara's charge slip from our local health institute was still inside. I opened the book at random and the first words I read were about an immortal East Indian avatar named Babaji. The picture of the guru looked like a male version of Katherine.

Interesting coincidence, I thought.

I read the section about Babaji, then put the book down and picked up *The Initiation* by Donald Schnell. The book was signed, "For Richard, How can I thank you enough for guidance through the years. Warm Regards, Donald Schnell." He added his e-mail address. I recalled that my son Scott had given the book to me last year. He said the author had dropped it off at his "Malibu Shaman" metaphysical store. He wanted Scott to pass the book on to me. Receiving so many books, I had never opened it.

As I read the foreword, on the fourth line Babaji's name appeared again. The whole book was about Schnell's trip to India and his contact with Babaji and the transformation that followed. Supposedly Babaji is thousands of years old, and he simply manifests a new body every few years, so he always looks to be in his mid-twenties. And there is nowhere you go to see him. He might come to you, but you can't go find him.

This was far beyond coincidence. I decided Babaji was making his presence known.

The next day, when I sent Katherine an e-mail explaining what had happened, she responded with this:

Blessings

I am not here to convince you of anything.
I am not here to be recognized.
I am not a show nor an entertainment.
I am only here to serve.
I am only here to share my message
of truth, simplicity, love, and service.
I am no-one.
I am no-thing.
I am always with you.
BABAJI

Shortly after my Babaji experience, Tara did an astrological chart on Katherine:

> In her past life, she was born with considerable artistic power, but her parents parted or something happened to them. I think she was an orphan—maybe royalty—and taken away and hidden somewhere.
>
> In this life, she has odd but wonderful karma. Her face to the world reflects honor, intelligence, eloquence, and fulfillment. She will always find the energy to accomplish what she wants to do. Popularity, individuality, and glamour sit on her Mars. She is well prepared for the work she has to do, and the only thing she needs to worry about is overdoing.
>
> Sometimes she feels blocked, but this is her chart holding her back until she properly prepares to move on. It will be her creative actions that make her money, and she will have wealth. In the least, she will be rich in life.
>
> Katherine's Saturn is tied to communication skills. She has popularity, harmony, and activity sitting here. She knows how to talk, what to talk about. At times, she gets very uncomfortable with people. People can overwhelm Katherine with their confused responses, their superficial observances or actions. Surrounded by many people, she needs alone time, creative time to recuperate. She has a lot of social standing in the Third House of communication, and she will experience unusual events, which will help her move forward in that area. In the area of soul goals, she incarnated to draw upon past artistic abilities once again.
>
> Katherine needs a lot of security around her emotional life. She feels as if she owes her relationship partners something. It is imperative these partners and her friends are emotionally supportive so she can concentrate on her creativity. Surprises will be big when they happen in the area of creativity, and it will always be creativity that drives her forward. Her artistic ability sits in Libra, and it's all about beauty and balance. She has a focus for business, and she likes to be in business with people she loves or admires for their talents.

Life is very fast and hard for her due to a Sun opposition to Pluto. Pluto moves you forward to wherever you want to go in life. Her Pluto emphasizes, again, beauty and art. A job providing Katherine the opportunity to move around is ideal for her. This woman needs to be busy.

Something unusual is upcoming in her career. I see double luck. She doesn't always get what she wants, but she will get what she needs. There are many changes upcoming: changes, changes, changes. She needs to avoid being too emotionally attached to anything she does.

Katherine goes back and forth on changes. This is her Gemini rising—should I, shouldn't I? She feels unsure, but she just needs to test the waters and if it feels good to her, go forward. She has keen perception. She can use her intuition to feel things out and decide if they will be good for her.

In the area of higher knowledge, publishing, the occult, Katherine's success is indicated for anything intense and emotional. Anything she creates for the public—books, scripts, films—this is her karma. She loves to create, but her work must be something of depth.

Her Midheaven, which is her Dharma, her career, is tied to Arcturus, which is a Persian Royal Star. Overall, she will get what she wants in this lifetime, because Spica and Arcturus will see to it. Her Sun and Moon midpoint also sit on the Midheaven, which says this is where she ultimately wanted to be. On a soul level, she knew she would give up her true parents in this life, because she knew her journey would take her to where she wanted to go creatively. Her parents were not there for her in her past life either. Her Midheaven also supplies her with an assertiveness to get what she needs. She will always be heard. And people will love her and see her as a spiritual person. The love she brings to others is from a spiritual position that is the most powerful aspect of all 360 degrees of the astrological chart.

Katherine cannot be anything but intense. She is very serious about life, and she will fulfill her missions. I say missions, because she is not to get too wrapped up with one cause. In relationships, she goes into a very intense emotional mode. From what I see here, in a past life she was not allowed to have a relationship. She was married to someone she didn't love—an arranged marriage of royalty. She was not allowed to know love and was probably abused by the man. Abused emotionally. She experienced a life of material abundance but had no freedom.[2]

Tara ended her reading by saying, "Within two years Kathcrine will get a lot of what she wants, and within five years her life will reach a beautiful apex."

In summary, Babaji predicted: "This year is going to be an amazing year. This is a year of transition. There will be two huge projects."

As I finalize this writing 13 months later, I can tell you how Katherine's year turned out. In the months following the hypnosis session, MTV asked her to direct one of its top-rated shows, *The Real World*. She accepted the offer and was so good that they asked her to direct a new show to be called *The Newlyweds,* a reality show, which was to observe real-life newlyweds Jessica Simpson and Nick Lachey. Katherine captured intimate moments that became media fodder. The show exploded, becoming successful beyond anyone's expectations. Directing also meant constant travel, following the "newlyweds" on tour, vacation, and media appearances. After directing two seasons, Katherine turned down an offer to direct the third season so she could work on producing a film she has written.

To top off the year, Katherine also fell in love and she and her lover are currently buying a home in Los Angeles. Babaji either foresaw what was to come or he had a part in manifesting the outcomes.

8

Donald Schnell

"One often meets his destiny on the very road he took to escape it."

—La Fontaine, French writer

In the previous Katherine Brooks chapter, I mentioned Donald Schnell, author of *The Initiation*—a story of Donald's experience in India with Babaji. Upon finding a personal dedication in the front of the book, I sent him an e-mail apologizing for not saying thank you, told him I enjoyed the book, and explained the unusual circumstances of Katherine channeling Babaji, and how I "accidentally" picked up his book the following day. Donald responded, and we talked about meeting for lunch. It took us five months to get together, but before I relate the outcome of our meeting, I will share some of Donald's story.

The Initiation begins, "Have you ever heard of Babaji? The flower children of the sixties know Babaji as the mysterious figure sitting in lotus posture and floating above all the notables on the cover of the Beatles' *Sergeant Pepper* album. Babaji is known to the spiritual seekers of India as the *deathless Maha-Avatar. Maha* is a Sanskrit descriptor, which literally means 'mega.' *Avatar,* also Sanskrit, means 'the descent of Divinity into flesh.' It is recorded that Babaji is the immortal Yogi-Christ/Buddha who works for the spiritual salvation of this age. It is said that he never openly appears in any century."

So you cannot go visit Babaji . . . because no one knows where to find him. If you are meant to meet, he will draw you to him.

When he was eight years old, growing up in the 1960s, Donald recalls studying a portrait of Babaji in Paramahansa Yogananda's classic *Autobiography of a Yogi.* The book was in his father's library. "I sincerely prayed to him, believing if I did so, he would respond," Donald said.

Thirty-four years later, in November 1997, Donald had long forgotten this prayer when he answered an urgent telepathic call to go to India, from his guru, Swami Nagananda. After spending several days with Swami, the guru told him, "Go away now and travel. Do not stay anywhere for more than 48 hours. Come back on December 25, and I will initiate you into the Swami Order."

Donald felt this made sense for he had dedicated many, many years to spiritual devotion. Following Swami's instructions, he left the temple in a taxicab driven by a young man named Babu. After a grueling seven-hour sightseeing trip, they stopped at a remote temple where Donald hoped to find a bathroom. Babu got out of the taxi and approached men guarding the gated temple entrance. Moments later he returned to the cab and excitedly explained that a highly evolved spiritual master called "Babaji" had arrived hours before and was in residence. Donald did not immediately connect the name to *The* Babaji—the immortal he had prayed to as a child.

> **From *The Initiation:*** After hours of sitting cramped, I ambled stiffly over to the gate. I noticed in the distance that a young man in a white robe was standing on the steps of the temple, waving to me as if to an old friend. He motioned for me to come in through the gate. About a score of Indian men stood or sat near him at the entrance to the temple. I waved back—not knowing whom I was waving to.

Donald took a moment to gather his things from the cab, and by the time he returned to the gate the friendly man was a great distance away, now sitting beneath a banyan tree across the compound. Donald was shaken, not understanding how anyone could have covered such a distance in such a short time.

I could feel waves of spiritual vibrations coming from the young man in white. It was as if he were a fountain sending forth streams of spiritual nourishment to the surrounding area. Even the usual cackling crows and chittering monkeys were quiet. I approached slowly, as if being pulled by a conveyor belt. I wasn't aware of walking. My muscles somehow found the ability to move on their own. Our eyes connected with a oneness, and what I'm relating here was taking place through this shared vision. I was seeing him see me as he was seeing me see him. It was like an infinite mirrored image—a mirror bouncing off a mirror bouncing off a mirror. My body took on the quiet demeanor of sleep. There was no longer the impatient need for water, nor was my body signaling the urgent need of a restroom. There was a transcendental reality—somewhat like sleep—that was beyond the physical body and mind and the perception of what was taking place. This isn't as strange as it sounds. It is typical to be unaware of bodily demands during deep sleep. We even lose awareness of the pain of a terrible toothache when we fall into a state of peaceful sleep, where there are no difficulties.

I was experiencing the Hindu teaching of *Maya*—the world as illusion—a projection from the mind. Just as a spider spins a web for itself, this world is spun from our ego and mind. Nothing else existed but this moment and those incredible eyes. I bowed reverently at the feet of this mysterious master and sat in a cross-legged position in front of him.

Babaji acknowledged Donald as "Swamiji." Only that morning Donald's guru had informed him of his forthcoming initiation as a swami. How could Babaji know? Donald's head reeled, and he silently asked himself if this could be the Babaji that he prayed to as child.

"Yes, yes, I am that very Baba," he replied, in answer to my unspoken question.

A lengthy conversation followed. Babaji talked about Donald's wife, Marilyn, and her children. He told Donald he would never see his mother again on the Earth plane, and he predicted upcoming worldly events.

"It is your Dharma to bring new spirituality to a new era," Babaji said. "Teach meditation for rejuvenation of its followers. Meditation will bring real peace to the planet because it will not be words, but rather the true experience of peaceful divinity that blossoms in the practitioners. The young in body and the young at heart want to experience God. When we think old, then God is far away. I will send you the sweet people."

In response to Donald's question about what he was to do, Babaji replied:

"Fill your day with *prema, shantih,* and *ahimsa*—with love, peace, and nonviolence. Fast, eat living foods, and it will be easier for you. Together, you and Marilyn will guide many to this high spiritual choice. Be prepared for me to come to you often, not only to come to you, but to come *as* you."

As Donald continued to relate his experience, the verbal exchanges with the Avatar were fascinating. Babaji initiates Donald, and the reader realizes he will be changed forever.

Before proceeding on his journey, Donald returned to where he began this life-changing day—the city of Bangalore. He agreed to separate from his driver, Babu, for only a few minutes while he ran to his room to freshen up. Then they were to go to the bank, so Donald could pay Babu before they set off on another journey. But less than 30 minutes later, when Donald returned from his room and asked the hotel doorman to locate his driver, he was presented with an older man named Babu.

"No, I want the *young* Babu driver," Donald insists.

"We only have one Babu here," replied the doorman.

The young Babu never turned up to claim the equivalent of $300, enough for an Indian family to live on for months. Was the driver real? Was the driver Babaji or one of his helpers?

Donald began to experience major personality changes. Others recognized him as a swami, and he now had the power to heal. Indian people lined up on the streets to experience his touch and blessings.

On December 24, the night before his formal initiation with Swami Naganunda, Donald could not sleep, and looked back over his life. "I saw my early childhood as a motherless twin, my grade-school self, and the endless fistfights with the mining town bullies. I saw the young teen sweating in the copper mine, the Eagle Scout, the financially strapped college student, and the zealous born-again Christian. I saw my medaled military years, my fellow soldiers embracing me as their *roshi* in the Zen Buddhist tradition. I saw the martial artist, the trained runner, the bodybuilder enthusiast, the hatha yoga and meditation teacher. I saw the young married man, managing a spiritual center, the dedicated schoolteacher, the lover, the adulterer, the mystic, the graduate student in higher education. I saw chiropractic school and the struggle to compete as an older student with a family, holding down two part-time jobs; the twice-divorced man; the brokenhearted father; the materializing guru; the writer; the published author; the lecturer; and on and on. And I was saying good-bye to all of them."

Donald was initiated Prema Baba Swamiji.

Prema Baba Swamiji, I said silently to myself, repeating my name for the first time since Babaji had given it to me weeks earlier. With so much going on, I wanted to make sure I wouldn't forget it.

When the ceremony was over Swami Nagananda walked Donald outside the temple.

"You will be a married swami," he said. "I brought you and Marilyn together, and nothing can separate you."

"The West needs a balanced approach to spirituality," Swami added. "They need the male and female, the Mother and the Father. I have one more gift to give."

Donald says:

Again, he whispered into my ear. This final blessing of the ceremony would remain my secret prophecy. It was time for me to leave. I was being instructed to return to the West, and to bring the blessings of Babaji's Swami Order to the millions of sweet souls thirsting for enlightenment.

Tara and I met Donald and his wife, Marilyn Diamond, for lunch at The Inn of the Seventh Ray, a vegetarian restaurant in Topanga Canyon. Donald, a handsome man in his mid-forties, dressed in casual California attire, did not look the part of a swami. Marilyn is a thin, beautiful woman, the mother of three grown children.

We found a secluded outdoor table in a gazebo. As it was summertime and fruits and vegetables were in abundance, Donald and Marilyn focused upon eating a raw-food diet. Tara and Marilyn perused the menu with Marilyn offering advice. I told Tara to choose for me. Marilyn coauthored *Fit for Life,* a 20-million-copy best-selling diet and lifestyle book. She has written other lifestyle titles on her own and *Fitonics* with Donald. While the ladies talked lunch options, I guided the conversation with Donald back to the ending of his book. Babaji had made it clear during the initiation that he would put Donald in a "yogic sleep" while he remade his body, mind, and personality to be his vehicle in the West. In the epilogue, Donald said, "He explained that the changes he was making would require about a year to complete in order for me to be the suitable ambassador for his message of divine love."

Marilyn laughed. "The process lasted two years." She shook her head and smiled lovingly at her husband. Upon Donald's return from India, Marilyn was waiting at the airport and was shocked at the sight of him in flowing orange robes, his stomach sticking out like a basketball—pregnant with enlightenment.

"Two years in a trance state?" I said.

Donald nodded and shrugged his shoulders. He returned from India changed in almost every way. He wanted only plant foods to eat and only one meal a day. His skin changed. He sequestered himself in his study to write and meditate. In time visitors came seeking his spiritual counsel and physical healings. He drove only when necessary and avoided freeways at all costs. He would often begin to spontaneously speak with an Indian accent and sometimes when lecturing he found himself channeling Babaji.

Our lunch extended for hours. We talked a great deal about their raw-food diet and the healing benefits they believed it offered. Tara and I enjoyed the time spent, and we left feeling as if we had made new friends.

The following day, Donald called and said, "I could hear the pain in your voice when you talked about your son's problem. I haven't done healing for a while, but I would like to work with him."

During lunch, Tara had explained that Hunter, our 17-year-old son, had alopecia areata, an unexplained loss of body hair. Although it was currently fashionable for teenage males to shave their heads, we felt he suffered psychologically as a result. We had worked for two years with top holistic and American Medical Association doctors in Southern California, without any resulting benefits for our son.

Donald, Hunter, and I met in my writing studio a few days later and Donald did adjustments and healing work on my son before talking to him about the importance of diet. "Food is medicine," Donald said, and he offered convincing case-history stories. "If you're willing to do a liver cleanse and eat only raw food for three weeks, I'll e-mail you the diet."

Much to my surprise, Hunter agreed. So I told him, "I'll do it with you. We'll go get whatever we need, and I'll fix the meals." At the time, Tara was in Montana and Utah with Emmy-Award-winning writer/director/editor Shane Stanley and Marla Maples, filming interviews with many Native American shamans for a new video project. With Tara away, I was handling meals for the kids, and I knew if I made it easy for my son, he would be more likely to stick to the diet.

When we were alone, Donald told me that he felt Hunter might have to make raw food a lifestyle to experience healing. We talked casually, and Donald said he had been using my tapes and CDs for years. As a hypnotherapist himself, he claimed to have modified my techniques to fit his style. I told him about the book I was writing and asked if he would be interested in doing some hypnosis work, maybe even contacting Babaji.

"Can we do it now?" he asked. I set up a lounger camp chair in my studio and directed him to begin deep breathing. A few minutes later, in a deep hypnotic sleep, Donald began speaking in a thick East Indian accent: "Doing, doing, doing. . . . Doing . . . Body still feels heavy . . . still has some weight to lose. But doing better."

I laughed, realizing Babaji was speaking and referring to Donald's already thin body.

"I hear your laughter," said Babaji. "And I know of you, and I bless your work. I'm thinking, who could come in human form? A God man. In the West, this is very difficult to understand, that God could appear in a human form. But I say to you, what mystery, what beauty, what magic, that God could appear as a woman. God could appear as a child. We can honor the flower, can we not also honor the human? Because the human is the greatest flower. So I say, see God in each other.

"It is not that I have some insight. I've been around for a long time. So I know less than anyone.[3] Because the older you get the less you know. The less you know, the less you need. Possessions are like coins in the pocket. The more of it you have, the heavier your pockets. I'm not saying that you can't enjoy things—material things—because enjoyment is God itself. But it's the attachment. These are things that you know, Dick. Can I call you Dick? These are things that you know, they're what you're teaching.

"You're not to be offended by what I'm saying. I bless the work. Blessing is what a swami does . . ." he chuckled, "it's what the yogis do. You notice the flower. A dog can go by the flower and miss it every time. The Swami Order was started because blessing energy is a way to uplift the human race. But it doesn't have to be in the form of a swami. It could come in many forms. The greatest work we do is blessing work . . . to step aside and let God come through to bless.

"Each individual is a sun, glowing bright. When the energy is high, the sun is high. It's automatic. Now there is something about your mother. It is something good, of course," he chuckled again. "Not something bad. Something good. And that goodness goes through you and goes through to everybody in your family. But the mind is thinking, thinking, thinking . . . we're not talking about the mind, I'm talking about the karma. There are obstacles, but the obstacles can be changed. And the blessing work I'm talking about is to change the karma. Karmas come from the mother and the father, but in this case the karma that we're talking about is coming from the mother. But it's not negative to blame the mom. It's not like that. It's the . . . stuff . . . the things.

"Babaji is a wish-fulfilling tree. When the world was created there were many plants, many trees . . . and there was Babaji. And the wish-fulfilling tree, when your karma is right, then Babaji comes. Always to bless . . . to take you to the next level. More joy. Can't we get there ourselves? Of course we can get there ourselves, but there is the short way and the long way (chuckling). The long way can be very, very long. So grace is a factor of the world. It is. You know. When Babaji comes into the grace . . . I'm looking at you now. I am seeing you listening and watching. Even with the eyes closed, I can see." (Donald's eyes were closed, but he turned his head toward me for a few moments.) "Sight is not limited to the eyes, sound is not limited to the ears, even the touch is not limited to the hands.

"Tara is going through some difficulty, but even this is changing. All is my will. Not to be afraid . . . I'm not some kind of dictator. You are Higher mind and Babaji sees. Bodies change. Higher mind, same. We're opening the doors to grace . . . with some difficulty . . . what already changes. We're servants of love. We're guided by love. Some are thinking that love is not wisdom. But love is the ultimate wisdom."

At this point in the session, Babaji seemed to just fade away, and Donald's voice came in weakly. "I'm sort of feeling halfway . . . like I'm halfway back . . . this is Donald . . . the hand position . . . in my right hand is his . . . he's moving my hand that way . . . it's sort of frozen. The yogis call it *amonda*. He's shifting out of my body space . . . and this hand is sort of frozen, too . . . the little finger is not. I open my eyes, I'm in trance . . . coming back. This is still frozen . . . I can move it, shake it . . . like that. I'm curious about it."

Donald awakened, and after a bathroom break, he told me he had looked in the mirror and the eyes looking back at him were not his own.

In a second hypnosis session, Babaji spoke through Donald once again, and mentioned my mother. I explained she was deceased and asked if he was perceiving her in spirit. As if in response to the question, Babaji evidently drew my mother to us and repeated her words. She wondered about the white in my hair and asked why I wasn't drawing, "You are so good at drawing, Dick."

My mother would have said something like this, because she loved me being an artist and art director, and never quite "got" my metaphysical callings.

In ending the session, I asked Babaji if he was open to future sessions, asking him questions, recording the responses, and sharing the wisdom in books and articles. He agreed.

Two days later, Hunter and I started the liver cleanse. Upon awakening I squeezed the juice of a fresh organic lemon into a cup and added two tablespoons of extra virgin olive oil in a glass of warm water. An hour later we drank two full glasses of organic grapefruit juice. We ate as many bananas as we wanted until lunch time, when we ate salads and fresh guacamole dipped with cucumber slices.

Hunter vowed to follow the diet for three weeks. After the first day, I wasn't so sure I wanted to do this, but I adapted. When Tara returned home, she eagerly embraced the liver cleanse and diet, which supported my own commitment. In three weeks, I lost ten pounds.

Hunter fulfilled his vow, and although he did not become a raw foodist, he ate more healthfully than he used to. Today, I eat far more raw food than I did before meeting Donald and Marilyn, and

Tara continues to push our diet in this direction. Donald suggests a diet consisting of 70 percent raw foods, which sounds like a good goal to me.

Considering my initial experiences with Don, and the fact I had been in direct contact with Babaji on two separate occasions, I wondered if I was experiencing synchronicity or was the Avatar intervening in my life for a reason? I preferred to think of it as synchronicity, because I had never been interested in attaching to a guru.

Swiss psychologist Carl Jung coined the term *synchronicity*, meaning the simultaneous occurrence of two meaningful but not causally connected events. One of the ways our soul pushes us in new directions is through synchronistic connections.

A hundred years ago, a scientist was staying in a house where two clocks always kept the exact same time—second to second. One clock was on the wall of the dining room, the other clock on the other side of the wall in the parlor. The scientist decided to set one of the clocks five minutes ahead. Within 24 hours, both clocks had aligned again. He conducted further experiments, but eventually both clocks would always align to the same rhythm. The man decided the vibration of the larger clock was feeding through the wall and keeping the smaller clock in tune—a subtle influencing.

Maybe a similar rhythm or energy generates a subtle influence causing people and things to be drawn together in meaningful ways, because our soul wants us to pay attention.

Upon listening to the tape of Babaji talking to me and hearing my communications with Donald, Tara was anxious to cast his astrological chart. Donald is an Aquarius Sun and Cancer Moon with a Scorpio Rising. Tara said:

> His recent past life appears to have been very fortunate. Although it might seem obvious, I do believe, based upon what I see here, he was an East Indian guru last time around.
>
> This life, he is surrounded by family and good fortune. He's intense and emotional and has popularity on his Saturn, which may cause him to go up and down a little in the area of popularity. In the area of security, he has good fortune with love and business. He is seen as a loving person, and increase and benefits

come to him through love and being loving. Assertiveness, dedication, and loyalty are strong factors here concerning love. Intelligence and skill come up again and again. He was born to communicate and interact with people. Being a perfectionist serves him as he walks into the future.

Notoriety in regard to creative projects is strong. Surprise and unusual events . . . he didn't really expect to end up where he is. Sudden and drastic changes are indicated. Some of them haven't been easy, but he intellectualizes changes as preparation for his mission.

Donald is very smart and quick-witted with prophetic instincts. Marriage suits him well. He has considerable Divine protection around him. His Pluto is in his ninth house of publishing. He is supposed to publish—the jet fuel in his life will come through publishing, resulting in praise and higher knowledge.

His service to mankind is harmony and interaction—the basic goal of his life—to center himself, go forward, and interact with others in harmony. Neptune sits in his house of groups, so his psychic ability is strong in this area. Any obstructions he feels with associations or groups are there only to build his strength to transform to be the one. The most intense aspect is guidance, which is probably Babaji. I thought this was beautiful, because Donald's divine guidance aspect is the most powerful aspect in this chart.

In summary: Donald's astrological chart mirrors his life today, and his soul contract is to bring "peaceful divinity" to the planet. But along the way, he had considerable karma to resolve and Dharma to fulfill, just like everyone else. I am intrigued with the preparatory lessons he had to experience prior to becoming Prema Baba Swamiji in his mid-forties. He was a zealous born-again Christian, military man, Zen Buddhist, martial artist, teacher, and a chiropractor who had two previous marriages. Everything we do in life is in some way preparing us for what we are destined to do.

Swami Nagananda said, "I brought you and Marilyn together, and nothing can separate you." Other avatars and swamis like Babaji and Sai Baba are also prone to this form of "assistance," which I find a bit bothersome, but I assume the help is in keeping with an individual's karma and the greater good of the planet. It is probably no different than your spirit guides or angels maneuvering you to be in the right place at the right time to meet someone who is destined to become important in your life. Marilyn's dietary awareness and Eastern wisdom are powerful support in the seminars the couples co-train and in their private counseling work.

Tara claims Donald was a guru in his last life, so he has returned to continue work started long ago. This time, he wanted to do it as a married American swami. As his life mission evolves, I hope he will tell us about the secret prophecy Swami Nagananda whispered in his ear after the initiation.

In the following chapter, I meet Babaji again, this time in Sedona, Arizona, when Donald manifests objects, and while hypnotizing medical intuitive Patti Conklin.

9

Patti Conklin

"Destiny commands, we must obey."
—Winston Churchill

I had heard about the phenomenal abilities of medical intuitive Patti Conklin for years before we met at the International Medical and Dental Hypnotherapy Conference in Detroit, Michigan, in October 2002. Upon shaking hands, I felt a reconnection with a very old friend. After the convention, Patti and I kept in touch via e-mail, and I asked her if she would co-train the participants in my Sedona Healing Seminar with me the following year. My wife, Tara, normally co-trained the seminar, but she was taking a year off the seminar circuit to work on her own writing and video projects. To my delight, Patti accepted my invitation.

We touched base again a few months later at the American Board of Hypnotherapy Convention in Newport Beach, California, where we were both conducting workshops.

I attended Patti's ABH luncheon lecture and was so impressed, I asked Tara to join me in Newport Beach for her post-convention workshop titled "Vibrational Medicine: The Healing Modality for Our Time." Being intuitive, my wife linked right into Patti's energy. While demonstrating a technique for drawing disease out of a middle-aged female participant and into her own body, Patti began to turn green. Not kind of green. Green. Tara experienced the intense energy draw, observed Patti's new color . . . and began to panic.

"I don't understand how anyone can do that on a regular basis," Tara whispered, after the demonstration. "I was sincerely afraid for her."

Patti explained that after drawing the woman's disease into her own body, she would now experience a physical purging for a couple of days.

"Patti would be a perfect case history for the *Soul Agreements* book," Tara said. "She's an angel, reincarnated to help save the planet."

A few months later, Patti and I were both presenters at another hypnosis conference. She invited Tara to bring our son, Hunter, to her all-day "Cellular Cleansing" process. Tara and our daughter, Cheyenne, accompanied Hunter to the cleansing to share the experience. Patti was surprised how much help Hunter required. She said she felt he had decided on moving to a higher level to work on his own healing, and that he had made the decision just in time, as he had been moving rapidly toward serious disease.

It took Patti several days to purge her body of what she had drawn out of Hunter. Within a few weeks, he began to grow a little more hair. And most noticeably, there was a change in attitude. After the time spent with Patti, he began expressing a much more positive view of life.

On Sunday night following the close of the conference, Patti was exhausted after working all day with individual clients. But Tara and I had dinner with her and her boyfriend Ajamu Ayinde, a transpersonal hypnotherapist. We talked about her work, my work, and the seminar we would co-train in Sedona in October.

By the time she was five, Patti was seeing angels and guides. She had thought they were human until she tried to hug one and her arms passed right through. She said, "I began to understand, deep inside me, that what I was seeing was truth and what my parents were telling me didn't exist, did exist—and they were wrong."

At age seven, Patti had a visitation. Before describing the incident, she wanted to explain that her perception of God was all-encompassing and that she doesn't attach the word to any particular belief system. "And I use the terms Creator, Father, and God interchangeably," she explained.

"Tell us about the visitation," I said.

"I was sitting in my bedroom and an incredible light began seeping through the walls. There was no being, only this phenomenal light, which generated an intense sense of humility in me. I went right down on my knees. There was no way I could not have gone down on my knees, and I bowed my head, because there was no way I could look up. And so I sat in that position for a few moments before hearing the most incredible voice begin speaking to me. Father said three things. He said that my greatest growth years would be from age 38 to age 42; that is when I would transform the most. Second, the years 42 to 62 would be my greatest giving to humanity—my period of greatest strength to do my work. And the third thing that I heard was something I did not understand. That my path and purpose in being here were to teach people to be insubstantial without transitioning."

Patti continued, "Even though I was a precocious seven-year-old, I did not know what that meant—to be insubstantial without transitioning. And that was the end of the visitation. From then on, I felt like I was living dual lives. I felt as though I was a normal child in every aspect, and yet there was a divided part of me that was much more spiritual than anyone around me. And I recognized that I was looking at life in a totally different way than my peers and my parents did. I also decided at this age that my dual life was not something to talk about openly."

As a young woman, Patti was driving by a psychiatric center when she heard Father tell her to stop, to go into the center, and to check herself in for three days. "You feel that you're different. They will tell you why you're different."

She did as instructed. The doctors accepted her admittance, and after running tests asked if she could stay longer. They decided she was not psychotic, but they wanted to investigate further. When the testing was complete, a psychiatrist told her, "If you think you're different from other people, it is because you are. Your mind processes 250 times faster than normal. You also have a genius IQ, which is your salvation. Without it, you would probably be psychotic."

Patti continued. "In my mid-twenties, I gave birth to two boys, each of whom shared part of my intuitive abilities. My oldest has the visionary capabilities. At two years old, he would climb into my bed in the middle of the night and tell me about an accident 250 miles away in which children had died going off a bridge. And the next morning it would be on the front page of the newspaper. My second son was born with energy capabilities unlike anything I had ever seen in children.

"By the time I reached my early thirties, I understood that the predicted transition was taking place. When I was 33, I woke up one morning and I had full sight. And it was the first time I had ever had a visitation in my dreams. God came to me in my dream and said, 'Soon I will lay the whole world before you. And I would like you to begin walking your path.' And when I woke up that morning, I looked at my then-boyfriend and just started screaming hysterically. I jumped out of bed, ran down the hallway to the kitchen, and just stood there gagging. It was awful. I was hysterical because I thought, 'Boy I've gone over the edge, I'm totally psychotic now.'

"As I stood in the kitchen, watching a little bird fly up to the bird feeder, I went from trembling to screaming again, because there were no feathers on that bird. Not a one. I could see its little heart beating and see its arteries flowing, and I could see the actual blood cells going through the blood. I could see it all in full color.

"I went back down to the bedroom, where Chuck was saying, 'What is your problem?' And I literally went in with my eyes turned away, and I laid my hands on his body because I could not see his flesh. I could see his skeletal structure: I could see the neurological structure, I could see the tendons, I could see the blood, I could see his teeth . . . I could see everything but his flesh.

"I'll tell you, every time the dog came up to me that day, I had a real problem. And by that night, I just lay down and said, 'Father, you know I've always done what you asked me to do. I've had visitations throughout my life telling me specifically where to live, who to be with; my life has been very much designated for me. I'm willing to do the work, but I really need an on-and-off switch, because I feel it is morally and ethically wrong to look through someone without their permission.' So the next morning, I had an on-and-off switch.

"During my 38th year, I worked as director of Canine Companions for Independence in Florida. But one day Father came to me and said, 'I want you to take the family and move to Hartwell, Georgia . . . and begin fully walking the path that I've asked you to walk.'"

"I didn't hesitate. I called my boss and resigned. He couldn't believe I was just going to leave. But to me there was no hesitation. When you started to analyze, you started having difficulties. So we sat down as a family. And I remember, specifically, Chuck saying to the boys, 'What do you guys think of this?' And Daniel, who was 14 at the time, said, 'If that's what Mom has been told, then that's what we do.'

"So we moved to Hartwell, and things began to change greatly for me. I began working with people, doing healings all over the country. And as a result of my work, I began to understand how someone could become insubstantial without transitioning. God was asking me to teach people how to clear the cellular body—everything you have stored in the actual cells of your body—so that *you can become divine without having to die to do it.*

"Wouldn't that be nice, to be in a place of no judgment, no ego, without having to die to do it. To begin to change the vibrations of this Earth . . . to begin to change so much of the horror that takes place around the world, just by utilizing our vibration?"

At this point, our discussion of Patti's background branched off into an exchange of philosophical ideas as to how we humans came to Earth as well as the concept of destiny.

"I believe that way back in time, God the Creator broke off billions and quadrillions of sparks in one event," Patti said. "And at that chosen time, every contract for every sojourn that we would experience was decided upon. *At that time.* And we began different sojourns—different life journeys whether it was here on Earth, Mars, Mercury, another galaxy, different forms, ETs, it doesn't matter. Each of those divine sparks began a journey. And for those who came here to Earth, we came as a very light Light-being. We came as that angel, that high-flowing, vibratory being. A Light Person. We came here, and we began to evolve. We created thought, which generated emotions. And as we began to experience emotions, we began to create lower vibrational emotions, such as anger, jealousy, resentment.

"As we created those vibrations, we began to become more dense. Because lower vibrations slow down the whole vibratory process. As we began creating a density, we had to create a chakra system in order to continue our energy flow. It was like we were being suffocated. Think of your vibratory system as a fast-spinning fan, the blades moving so fast you can't see them. Now if you throw enough molasses into those blades, you're eventually going to gunk it up and slow it down. And that's what we did with our bodies. We threw enough lower vibrations in there to begin gunking them up and we began to shut down our divine being. We began creating skin, flesh, bone. And being dense, we had to create a chakra system to keep our energy flow going.

"Throughout eternity we have continued to add lower vibrational emotions to our DNA structure. When we manage to get back to the point of being insubstantial without transitioning, we won't need our chakra system. They were an add-on. They're what keeps the energy field here. But in truth we should be working with a subtle energy."

Tara asked Patti how she perceived the heart chakra.

Patti replied, saying, "When I look at a heart chakra, I see the energy system of the heart chakra—a little glowing bit of whirling vibration. But if I look deeper in, beyond that heart chakra, I see the energy system, which is really a subtle energy field of what we should be. It's the yin and the yang. It's what we must keep in balance in order to maintain full health. Others would call it the immune system. To me it appears like a series of highways moving throughout the body. And every once in a while, you just get blocked spots, which in time manifest a condensed energy in your body that can create illness and disease.

"This is a part of the body we really need to work on. The third layer in what I term the personality of spirit. Now most people would term this the soul, or your Higher Self. Our soul is the personality of spirit, which goes back to all those gradrillions of sparks breaking off from source. It was then that you created your personality of spirit—who you became as a soul. It's a piece that is still attached to the divine, but it is not the divine spark itself. It is only a little tiny sliver of that.

"And if I go deeper into that personality of spirit, if I go through that layer and look deeper into the body, I see a deep, dark tunnel. And it holds all the fear you've ever experienced. It holds the shadow side of you. We all have it. And I don't care what level we get to, we all have it. The idea is not to try to get rid of it. We have to know duality. We don't know what good is without knowing what bad is. We don't know what light is without knowing dark. We can't get rid of it. What we really need to do is go inside and fully, unconditionally love it, because it is part of us. It is our perception that the shadow is wrong. Who is to say what is right or wrong? Isn't that where we get into judgment? What one person thinks is right, another thinks is wrong. And we begin this massive conflict.

"To me, the only thing that God asks of us is to love each other unconditionally. And that means without judgment and without ego. How do you do that? By fully accepting everyone for who they are. There are different contracts between God and all those zillions of sparks. You can't know what another person's contract is."

We ended our conversation talking about our personal lives and sharing experiences. Patti and I stayed in close contact over the summer and early fall via e-mail and phone. She called me one afternoon, saying my face had been right there in front of her all morning long.

"You're seeing visions of me way down in Hartwell, Georgia?" I said.

"I was worried and wanted to make sure you're okay."

I explained I had been dealing with an upsetting situation, but was amazed that I was projecting anxiety from Malibu all the way to Hartwell.

Our next meeting was in Sedona, Arizona, October 2003, where Patti would help me conduct my annual healing seminar. Sedona, with its red-rock mountain formations, is to me the most beautiful place on Earth. A 2003 poll conducted by *USA Today* newspaper came to the same conclusion. Sedona is also the location of powerful vortexes emitting intense energy from the Earth. Strange manifestations are almost ordinary here, because the vortexes intensify your own energy. Maybe your soul's vibrational rate increases here, allowing you to do now what will be common a few incarnations in the future.

There are four primary "power spots" in the world—two positive and two negative. Sedona and a remote location in Hawaii are the positive vortexes. The negative vortexes are in the Bermuda Triangle and Sussex County, England.

I had invited Don Schnell and Marilyn Diamond (from the previous chapter) to join us for the three-day-weekend seminar. And as it turned out, the seminar ended up being the most intense and inspiring training I had conducted in years. Tara joined me to conduct a group meditation. I conducted the Friday morning healing sessions and Patti took over in the afternoon. Following an exciting lecture, she pulled two people from the audience and conducted healings in which she drew the disease from their body into her own, freeing them of symptoms.

In addition to physical healing, one of the women required the fragment of herself at age two to be integrated. After this, the previously serious woman smiled and emitted childlike energy for the rest of the seminar.

Friday night, Patti, her boyfriend, Ajamu, and several of the participants we know to have healing abilities went to Airport Mesa vortex to focus our energy upon someone in great need of healing. Airport Mesa is my favorite healing location—the vortex I first wrote about in *Past Lives, Future Loves,* which introduced the world to the Sedona vortexes. San Diego hypnotherapist Steve Piccus led a visual meditation, Marilyn Diamond intoned a Babaji mantra to draw in the assistance of the "Immortal," and I conducted an energy process in which everyone placed their hands upon the subject and released energy into his body.

The next day he had a fever, which Patti attributed to the toxins being released. "After a healing, if the subject experiences a low-grade fever or flu-like symptoms, this is a good thing, for it shows the core issue has begun releasing," Patti said.

Saturday afternoon the participants visited energy vortexes of their choice. Tara and I went to the Red Rock Crossing area near Cathedral vortex with Patti, Ajamu, Marilyn, and Don. On the banks of Oak Creek, Don led us in a powerful meditation that included touch. I felt as if I left my body.

After being initiated as a swami by Babaji, Don became a healer in India. People lined up for blocks to await his touch. He also developed the power to manifest material objects, just like Babaji, Sai Baba, and other swami/mystics. During the afternoon, in response to Patti's use of the word "gold," Don began to tremble and shake his hand. We all watched as he manifested a gold coin. As the coin appeared, he said it was for our son Hunter, whom Don had been coaching on diet and healing. None of us had ever seen this done and we reacted in awe. That night he manifested a raisin, saying to me, "You need to be on raw food." I assumed this was another message from Babaji. Later that night, Tara and I split the raisin and ate it.

On Sunday morning, Tara conducted her "Medicine Woman" meditation. Then Patti did more individual healings before guiding a meditation in which she physically touched everyone in the seminar. Sunday afternoon, I followed this with the "group-focus" healing technique Tara and I have been using privately and with success in our Lake Arrowhead retreats.

Five seminar participants in need of physical healing were chosen. Next, eight to ten participants placed their hands upon each of the five subjects, and I directed the healing process. When it was over, a woman with a knee badly in need of an operation and another woman confined to a walker both stood up and started crying in joy upon realization of their mutual healing. They danced a jig together in front of the group.

The woman confined to a walker had had a hip-replacement operation that did not resolve her problem. After the jig, Patti continued the healing by laying her hands upon the woman's hip; she said she felt the metal literally melt and then snap into place.

To me, the seminar was a weekend of miracles, and I will share just one of the many letters and e-mails I received from the participants after it was over. The following is from Kim Harris, written a few days after the seminar:

I just returned from the Sedona Healing Seminar and would like to pass on my story of healing during this wonderful weekend.

For the last year and a half I have suffered from pain in the back of my head. It's not really a headache but more like pressure accompanied by constant throbbing. Even when I don't experience a lot of pain the area is sore to the touch. I had noticed that the pain began last year when I was appointed to a national committee for which I didn't feel qualified. Last year my doctor had me get an MRI but no problems showed up, so this pain was something I wanted to address during the seminar.

On Saturday afternoon I went to the Cathedral Rock area off Back O'Beyond Road and began with the healing meditation techniques that Dick had taught us. During meditation, I was taken to a past life where I worked for a close friend. I was shown a scene where he ordered me to do something that I considered morally or ethically wrong, so I refused. As a result, I was shot in the back of the head. During this meditation I wasn't shown what I had refused to do. I then used color as Patti had instructed to try and remove some of the pain that was coming from the area where I had been shot. This aspect of the afternoon became very emotional for me.

After Saturday afternoon, I was excited to find that the pressure pain was gone from the back of my head. Although the throbbing sensation remained, it was much more bearable now. On Sunday morning during Tara's meditation, I was told that in that past life, my "friend" had asked me to shoot and kill someone. When I had refused and was shot, I turned around to see that my friend was the one who shot me. He laughed as he told me that since I couldn't handle the job of killing for him, he had to get rid of me because I knew that he was killing others. As the meditation continued, I was able to resolve an issue regarding a lost friendship based on what had just been revealed to me.

When Patti came around to each of us during her last session on Sunday, she touched my heart chakra. When I awoke from that session, I felt so much lighter, like a huge weight had been lifted off my shoulders. Ever since then, the throbbing sensation at the back of my head has been gone, too! I have not had any more pain in my head, and it is no longer sore to the touch either. Had I manifested this old pain when I was appointed to the committee last year and felt unprepared and unable to handle the task?

Please accept my gratitude for the great seminar that Dick, Patti, and Tara conducted. I can't describe what a wonderful experience this was, but the fact that I came away from it pain-free is too incredible for words. *Keep up the wonderful healing work.* With many thanks, Kim Harris.

The day following the Sedona Healing Seminar, both Patti and I worked with individual clients all day. The evening had been set aside to do hypnosis explorations with Patti in our room at the Inn of Sedona. Following a relaxing dinner with Patti and Ajamu we all returned to the hotel. Tara agreed to do a chakra link with Patti and write what she perceived.

For my part, I wanted to ask Patti about a lot of things that I could only ask her under hypnosis. First and foremost, what had set up the current life of healing service. Second, I knew that when the Dalai Lama was speaking a few years ago, Patti had tried to get a ticket, but they were sold out. Hoping to hear his words anyway, she had stood in one of the passageways leading to the stage. She had not realized it was the passage the Dalai Lama would use to walk to the podium. As he passed Patti, he had stopped, bowed his head to her, and said, "It's so good to see you again, old friend."

When I had first heard the story, I asked Patti if she knew what the Dalai Lama meant. She did not, but she was open to exploring it in our hypnosis session. Patti made herself comfortable in a lounger chair, and she induced her own altered state of consciousness. I'd agreed to be a guide. My *Mind Converter* CD played low in the background to assist her in attaining a deep level. Once I felt she was ready, I said, "Talk to me about where you are."

Patti: "I seem to be floating . . . there are snow-capped mountains beneath me. I thought I was going to go out into the universe, but I didn't go there. Floating . . . like a cloud."

"Tap into your feelings. What do you feel?" I said.

Patti: "Curious. Observing."

"Are you within a period of time, or are you experiencing pre-time?"

Patti: "Pre-time. I don't think there are people. I'm not aware of souls here."

"But you are above the Earth?"

Patti: "Yes."

"All right, let's begin our explorations with the Dalai Lama's comment, which should ground you in space and time. When the Dalai Lama bowed to you and said, 'It's so good to see you again, old friend,' I believe he was referring to earthly time and space. If this is so, let's return to the period he was referring to. On the count of three, you will return to a time the two of you were together, if indeed you have known each other in another incarnation. One, two, three."

Patti sighed loudly, paused, and said, "I'm in a large room and many people are carrying candles."

"Is this part of a religious ceremony?"

Patti: "To give light. It's a big room . . . no windows . . . no natural light. They're not candles, more like torches, but small flames. I'm sitting in a big chair made of stone . . . and there is a young boy at my feet. This is the soul who is now the Dalai Lama."

"Where are you? What country?"

Patti: "It feels like what we now call Indonesia. It was not called that in 400 A.D."

"Since you're the one sitting upon the stone chair, I assume you are the deity or the leader? What role do you play for your people?"

Patti: "I would be considered a spiritual leader—the wise one. I'm male. It feels as through I am very well known throughout that land. I'm very old. My hands are all wrinkled. The people bring me food."

"What do you feel about being in this position of great responsibility?"

"Patti: "It simply is."

"Not something to be questioned? Do the people want to be touched by you?"

Patti: "Yes."

"Is this position your birthright, or did you earn it because of your leadership abilities, or your spiritual awareness?"

Patti: "It is what I have always been . . . who I have always been."

"A role you've repeated in many incarnations? All right, let's let go of this and move again in time. Have you shared an association in the past with Babaji? If so, you will move to that time and space on the count of three. One, two, three."

Patti sighed very loudly several times. When she didn't speak, I asked, "Are you and Babaji of the same energy?"

Patti: "The one you call Babaji has always been. And I can see him. I can see him, but we do not speak."

"Do you even need to speak?"

Patti: "No, I'm on my journey. I left much, but I wanted to know. When I wander I do not speak. I watch, and I learn. And he watches. And I watch him. I am the movement of him."

"You are the movement of Babaji?"

Patti: "I am the one whom people remember . . . the movement of him."

I realized I was talking to Patti in the past, but because of her level of awareness, I asked, "Is Don the movement of him as well?"

Patti: "A later movement. The same, but not of the same time."

"Are there many people upon the Earth who play this kind of role?"

She held up five fingers.

Patti: "There are five."

"So you have always done this work?"

Patti: "There have been many lifetimes of knowing. Babaji is the one and there are those who are the movement of him. I have taken many forms. Many that you remember."

"Would someone like Sai Baba be of the same energy?"

Patti: "He is separate. He is not of the movement."

"What can you tell me about the events of the last five days, where you say Don's vibration is akin to your own. To what purpose is this coming together?"

Patti: "There are different aspects of the movement who come over . . . over and over again. And sometimes we walk together . . . sometimes we walk separately. And this time has been a coming together. But Don has taken many shapes and forms. He has been, as I have been . . . we are the movement, the physical. We are the ones who touch. And we watch. But it feels as though the movement is faster, not in vibrations, but in observations. They no longer sit and are that to which people come."

"Can you further explain this?"

Patti: "When I gave up all worldly goods, I wandered. I walked and I walked, and I watched. And for a long time I was silent. Then I began speaking, and people would stop to listen to my words. And people began putting my words in form . . . writing. Over my many trips here, I've always been the movement for people to come to."

"Yet you are here in a physical body, having to accept physical challenges, just like everyone else. Obviously, this is the role you've chosen to play. From your current level of consciousness, can you communicate information your physical self needs to know?"

Patti: "This female form is very difficult. It is not of my experience. And this female form needs more of the facilitating food. More of the greens that grow on the Earth. More fasting."

Noting that Patti had switched viewpoints, I asked, "Is Babaji speaking through you or is Patti speaking?"

Patti: "The one that in the beginning created the movement. The first of the movement in form . . . is here. And I came into being here, within this space, with solid ground beneath my feet and a form to feel. You know me by many names."

"How have I known you before?"

Patti: "Many times. Many times. In the room . . . the big room, the one you now call Dalai Lama was at my feet. You stood to my left. You stood upon this land. And so many times you have been my advisor. The one who could hear . . . the thoughts and voices of the people. And you would take my words out to the people. Many, many times you've been there."

"Am I personally supposed to move in a new direction at this time? Is the contact with you, and Donald and Babaji . . . is there a purpose? What's going on?"

Patti: "The path is expanding. You will be walking in areas you have not walked in many lifetimes. In about three months of your time, you will begin broadening the path you now walk. You'll continue your vibrational shift as you know it. And many great miracles will happen for you. As you, yourself, continue . . . you will create. The advisor is always necessary. The advisor creates the synchronicity."

Patti paused, then continued, "Allow yourself to continue to trust. Be guided by him, and you will move into your rightful place. Look for the full moon in three months' time. A rebirthing will begin. You will begin to know. It will be more clear to you."

"How about Patti? I'm speaking to you, but also to an essence . . . an energy . . . a vibration beyond you. Where does Patti need to go now? Is there a new direction upcoming for her?"

Patti: "Yes, in approximately the same time period, there will be a much more challenging shift for her. It will not feel comfortable, but it will be necessary."

"Can you tell me about the work Ajamu is destined to be doing?"

Patti: "He is an orator. And his orations will grow. He will speak clearly. He will find his strength. It will grow within. His confidence and strength will grow very rapidly. His voice will be heard, yet his gentleness and humility will continue to be."

"Here we are working with you, and yet we're using you as the oracle. I hope this is okay. What about Tara's path? Is there anything you can share?"

Patti: "She will continue to grow. She is a tremendous light. She is very much looked upon by women as an essence of strength. What ego is left will continue to lessen . . . and her light will continue to shine. She has a great path . . . and a great responsibility. She is of Mother Earth. And the essence that she provides is of that. Then as we go through time, more and more people will need this essence of feeling from her. And her tasks will be great as she continues to grow. People will feel her acceptance and love. She is of this Earth and carries that with her. And while she may struggle for her identity, she has carried it for many lifetimes, and she will continue to do so."

I awakened Patti, because she had been in an altered state a very long time. We discussed the fact that over the last few weeks, she had not been able to easily throw off some of the diseases she has been drawing out of people. In the seminar, she extracted a head cold from a female participant, but now had the sniffles herself. Last week, she extracted herpes from a client, and now she was experiencing a breakout. She claimed there would be no trace of this disease in her body within a day or so, but she wondered why she didn't immediately toss it off as she usually did.

We decided to do another hypnosis session, returning to the awareness I had been communicating to in the first session. Once she was in a deep altered state, I said, "I'm interested in why Patti has not been able to toss off all of the sludge she extracts from others, as she has done in the past. Is this a cumulative reaction resulting from the work she is doing, or is she doing something that is blocking her ability?"

Patti: "She spends too much time in thought. She needs to be within the movement. She experiences sadness over a past parting and that's what causes her body to be stagnant. She needs to free her mind of thought. Be in the movement. Drink more water. It will correct easily."

"How does she still her mind of thought? She is of earthly body, so she is going to experience the desires and sorrows of the Earth plane. What can she do?"

Patti: "This one needs more discipline and trust. Her faith runs deep, but her trust does not."

"She will understand this?"

Patti: "Yes. Let's come back now."

I counted her up with positive, energizing, and healing suggestions.[4]

Tara sat behind me during the hypnosis sessions and occasionally pulled herself up out of trance to write a question, which she passed on to me to ask Patti during the session.

She wrote in her notebook:

> Dalai Lama—gold and dark, mauve walls. She is a male priest, much revered and a little bored. He wants to be of more service. The bureaucratic environment is trying. He loves the young boy but fears for his continued safety. They are children and priests of a war-torn country. He goes before the people and they want him to touch them. But he can only touch a few. He (Patti) has always been in the temple. As a young child, he had

no parents, never saw his family. He belonged to the society of priests and temples.

Patti has been Babaji's son. He went on to marry Mahurindu and she bore him nine children. He helped many with his gifts. He served the world, but he always sent his wife love and devotion. Patti carries many gifts from this lineage of Masters.

This writing was short, because when Babaji began speaking through Patti, Tara seemed to have been shaken out of the chakra link and awakened. I don't know why this occurred.

Shortly after our time together in Sedona, Tara drew up the following astrological information on Patti:

She is a Leo Sun, Gemini Moon, and Scorpio Rising. Based upon what I see here, Patti was a psychic priest in her last life, and I believe she became too famous and powerful—too well liked by the masses. She was killed for this, although a head priest may have made it look like suicide. I get strongly that she was Catholic and this occurred in Brazil.

She was forced to become self-sufficient due to leaving home at an early age, and also due to the men in her life. Now she can stand on her own and handle becoming more and more famous, which is her karma and Dharma. She will always be seen as a loving person doing glamorous work. People also view her as religious, optimistic, and truthful. And there will always be people who will come to her aid. There's a lot of happiness in this chart. She is obviously a caregiver, but in such an unusual way. The more she gives out, the more people will come to her, guiding her work to greater status. She'll be a mentor to many.

In this life, she has attained what she had in the past life as a famous priest. Drawing upon this energy, her speaking abilities came to the fore. It is something she has contracted to do. Her artistic ability, which I feel is her psychic and hands-on healing ability, is all there to help others. Overall she is happy in fulfilling this soul goal, which will influence many, many people. Her astrology says she has it all.

Patti's Midheaven, her service to others, indicates the occult. Her problems in childhood made her strong enough to do this work. People try to suck the life out of her, and few souls could withstand this. Sun and Midheaven conjunct says she will offer her work to the world. Pluto sits right next to her Sun in the tenth house, which means that she will become more and more famous. Her good fortune is also there and conjunct her Pluto. Plus Mars is also conjunct, so she will always be divinely taken care of. Always.

Over and over, I'm reading strong passions. A passionate, beautiful, giving, and charitable person. She sometimes feels locked up by doing her Dharma, but it was her choice. She needs to continue doing group work as well as her individual healings. The most intense aspect in her chart is her influence over others. She can influence the destiny of others.

In summary: I agree with Tara that "Patti is an angel reincarnated to help save the planet." In short, she made a soul contract to heal and educate. At the same time, she has taken on the mantle of a physical body, so she is subject to human emotions and problems just as you and I are. She also maintains a demanding travel schedule and accepts great responsibility. I was happy to hear recently that she is in the process of training other talented people to do supportive healing work. Patti also manages to produce a Web radio show once a week, even when traveling (see contacts in the back of the book).

Patti said in the hypnosis session that I would notice a shift in my life after the full moon in three months' time. At that time, I began to seriously work on this book, which I had been putting off for two years. Speaking offers began to come in from around the world, and I committed to an abundance of workshops, including more healing seminars with Patti.

The hypnosis session with Patti marked my third contact with Babaji in eight months. I do not yet know, and may never know, the importance of the contact or what has changed in my life as a result. Maybe Babaji wanted me to share these stories in this volume, because the words will generate action by some readers.

I feel there is much yet to explore with Patti when we get together at various conventions and New Age expos, so I'll probably be meeting Babaji again soon. Donald Schnell and I also plan to further explore with Babaji.

Richard Christian Matheson and Diana Mullen

"Destiny has more resources than the most imaginative composer of fiction."

—Frank Frankfort Moore, author

The author copy on the flyleaf of Richard Christian Matheson's short story collection, *Dystopia,* reads, "a screenwriter, producer, director, and author of the critically acclaimed novel *Created By.* He is also a professional drummer and has worked as a parapsychological researcher."

That is the short, short version of Richard's career. He has written a dozen theatrical, cable, and network films, as well as miniseries, and in his younger days he scripted and produced hundreds of series TV shows. *Variety,* the Hollywood trade paper, labeled him "King of the Spec Script Writers" because he has sold so many original screenplays. The *San Francisco Chronicle* calls his fiction writing, "Quick-jab-to-the-viscera style . . . brilliant." *Rolling Stone* magazine says he is "one of a handful of resourceful, fear-minded authors helping to create a new sensibility in horror fiction that is as frightening and merciless as the modern world itself."

Richard plays drums in a band called Smash-Cut—a favorite in Hollywood clubs—and at one time played with "The Rock Bottom Remainders," a rock band made up of leading writers, including Stephen King. They play occasionally at publishing and writer's conferences. Richard also studied privately with legendary CREAM drummer Ginger Baker.

Through an introduction to the UCLA parapsychology department, Richard was part of the team researching the poltergeist manifestation case eventually depicted in the film *The Entity*. Today, his books, scripts, and short stories often reveal in-depth awareness of the occult.

In 1990, I took a break from my metaphysical communications to write a dark-fantasy book nominated by Horror Writers of American for a Bram Stoker Award. Tara and I attended the Nashville, Tennessee, conference and awards ceremony, figuring we would be outsiders in a world of strange people. As it turned out, horror writers are some of the nicest, most normal people we had ever met.

Richard introduced himself and his wife, Marie. They, too, lived in Malibu, and upon returning home we began meeting them for dinners and long evenings of stimulating espresso-fueled conversations. I am usually the one asking questions and driving conversations, but Richard outdid me many times over. I most enjoyed his quick wit and ability to make Tara and me laugh until our heads hurt.

Over the 1991 Christmas holiday, we met at our home for an evening gathering that turned into an impromptu nine-day party. Other friends and family wandered in and out, but the core group did not part other than to buy groceries, feed a cat, or get clean clothes. Tara cooked what she called "army-style" food, and we all slept on couches or in sleeping bags on the living- and TV-room floors. No one drank anything but espresso, so we could remain awake for more talking and to watch Academy Award screeners (tapes of new movies sent to Motion Picture Academy of America members). Similar unplanned gatherings followed over the years, but we have never topped those bonding nine days.

As Richard and I became close friends, we advised and counseled each other regarding writing and publishing strategies. If either of us found ourselves in personal conflict, we could count on the other to provide support and positive advice. When Richard and Marie divorced, Tara and I suffered along with them. We remained close to both as they healed and eventually went on to establish new relationships.

In 2001, Richard introduced us to Diana Mullen, a beautiful blonde New Yorker he had met during book-promotion travels. I loved her big smile, warm manner, and the easy conversation we experienced. Tara embraced her as well.

Diana worked in film production, had a holistic health background, and, like Richard, embraced all things metaphysical. We found no shortage of things to talk about.

In December of 2004, I sent e-mail invitations to nearby friends for Tara's birthday slumber party at our second home in Lake Arrowhead, California. "Bring food and a sleeping bag," the invite read. We planned to spend the weekend gathered around the fireplace, eating well, drinking espresso, talking, and watching movies—Tara's favorite kind of gathering. Few people are willing to brave the mountain in winter, and when the weatherman predicted a snowstorm, we doubted anyone would show. Tara and I arrived in Arrowhead the night before the party to find low-blowing snow whipping through the pines and gathering on the ground. My four-wheel-drive Land Rover slid uneasily on glazed-ice roads. Only Richard and Diana and one of Tara's girlfriends were brave enough to make the journey. The five of us had a laugh-filled weekend, and we found out we could no longer drink excess espresso without heartburn. Tara said, "We've all become wimps."

"Because we can't stay up all night without caffeine fuel?"

"Yeaaaaahhhhh," she said.

When the opportunity came up to do past-life regressions, I jumped at the chance to find a case history dramatizing how current-life interests could manifest in the next life. In Richard's case, what prerequisite experiences did he have in preparation for a life as a successful writer? And if we had time, I also wanted to explore what inspired his musical talents.

I induced hypnosis, and when Richard stepped out of the past-life time tunnel, he perceived himself as a little boy in a park with his grandfather. "There's a lake, stone bridge, boats floating through. There are people walking, sitting on benches, pushing baby carriages," he said.

In response to a question about his grandfather, Richard said, "He's overdressed. Too many clothes for such a warm day. An overcoat and hat with a walking stick—a cane. He smiles when I come up. He tells me it's time to go."

Back in their apartment, his grandfather fixed a meal for the two of them. Richard described their living quarters as "small, simple, and clean. We're in the kitchen. There's a stove and a musical instrument on the wall: a lyre, painted the way they paint things in Sweden."

"Does your grandfather play this instrument?"

Richard: "I believe my grandmother played it."

I directed him to move forward in time until something important happened.

Richard: "I'm in the library, and there's a girl reading on the other side of the table. We're both about 16. I'm peeking at her. She's peeking at me. She seems very shy. I don't think she is really reading the book. It's like a prop. And she gets up and goes upstairs. I follow. This is a big library. She's looking for other books in a quiet part of the library. I come up and pretend like I'm looking for a book, too. I smile, and we meet, and she tells me her brother just died. She is still mourning. She came to the library to be alone, but she smiles a little."

"All right, if a relationship develops, let's move forward in time to explore how this unfolds."

Richard: "We're in a bathtub, taking a bath together. I'm laughing. There are lots of suds—bubbles. We're in somebody's bathroom, but I don't know whose bathroom it is. But someone is banging on the door. It's a very nice bathroom, but they don't want us in there. I think months have passed since we met in the library. Maybe a year."

We established they lived in Connecticut in 1922, and the relationship with the girl continued. We explored glimpses of their life, including work at a newspaper. Richard is age 33 when he explains, "We're married now, and we both work in a big newspaper office. I lay out the articles and photographs. I don't write, but I would like to. There is a writer that comes in, and he seems very odd to me— very interesting to me. He's older. He seems like he knows a lot. He's seen a lot of painful things, and there is something about him that seems wise. I'm interested in him, but he ignores me. He comes in and drops things off. I don't think he works here. I'm aware of him, but I don't think he is aware of me."

"What does your wife do on the paper?"

Richard: "Jeanine works downstairs in the reception area, where the people come in. She doesn't like it. She's very, very, very bored. We have lunch everyday together—a place we like to go. She's pregnant and hungry, and she eats off my plate, too. We make a joke about that. The writer comes by and he looks in the window at us. There is no expression on his face. Strange. And she says, 'Maybe he is aware of you.'"

"Are you working to become a writer?"

Richard: "I don't even think about it, but he is so interesting to me. It's like I want to be him, but I don't want to be him. He's bigger than life and very mysterious. He's sad. He must be 60. He's gray. It's like everything he knows, he knows because it came from something sad. But he knows so much more than I know."

"Let's move forward to a time when your baby is here."

Richard: "A little girl, Mary, and she's riding a tricycle. Curly blond hair, a very happy little girl. We live in a little . . . like a walk-up, not much, very simple. I think this is the same place I was as a young boy with my grandfather. I see the lyre on the wall."

We established that Richard walks to his job at the newspaper, "But in the winter it is hard to get there," he says. In moving forward a few years, he found himself helping his daughter with her schoolwork. "I like this, I like the feeling of writing something down like that. She's not interested in doing her schoolwork. She has no focus. I try to get her to pay attention, but she's very playful . . . she's giggling. When I make her laugh, she loses her concentration. So I write this paper and get involved. It's just a report for a kid, and Jeanine comes in, and she teases me about it."

"Does Jeanine work at the paper, or does she stay home with Mary?"

Richard: "No . . . she started to bleed one day in the lobby, something about the pregnancy. And she didn't work after that. She stays home, she sews, she does things to make money. Cooks things for people, bakes things for people."

I directed Richard to move several years into the future, and to stop when he came to something interesting.

Richard: "I'm up in huge pine tree, way up. I look down and I see Jeanine in a wheelchair."

"What are you doing in the tree?"

Richard: "I'm hiding from Mary. I'm making it sound like the tree can talk . . . and she's laughing, Jeanine is laughing."

"Why is Jeanine in a wheelchair?"

Richard: "She was hit by a car on the street, and she could never walk again. Mary and I like to make her laugh."

"How old is Mary now?"

Richard: "Thirteen."

"Do you continue to work at the newspaper?"

Richard: "No, I teach at school. Somebody Jeanine knew helped me get the position at the school. It's fifth grade, and I teach English. A small class of a dozen students. We read and do book reports. At night I read with Mary and Jeanine. And there are papers to correct. Sometimes I miss the newspaper, I miss all the people. It's a lonely life."

"Are you fairly content? You have your wife and child."

Richard: "Yes. We don't have much money, but we get by."

I directed Richard to move forward to the last day of his life in this past life we were examining. "No pain, no emotion, and on the count of three you'll be there. One, two, three."

Richard: "We're on the beach by a lake. We're lying on towels. Mary is swimming with her boyfriend. Jeanine and I are lying there in the sun. And I just get very tired . . . and it feels as if I'm almost sinking into the sand . . . but it's nice, it's not a bad time."

I directed him to move forward into spirit, just a few moments after leaving his physical body. "Can you see the body you just left? What is happening?"

Richard: "People are gathered around, and Mary's boyfriend tries to revive me. Other people from the lake come around. Crying. I don't really want to watch this . . ."

I returned Richard to the present, but asked him to remain in a relaxed altered state. "I would like to continue to examine your past, by exploring the origins of your love of music and your musical talents. Let's move through time, to explore any predominate musical influences, especially a lifetime influencing drumming."

Richard: "I'm an engineer on a train, and we move through the night. I love the sound of the train, moving on the tracks, the sounds of the wheels moving, the rhythm. The repetition of the sounds going through a tunnel. I love that. All the sounds. The percussion of it. Everything, putting the wood in the . . . the whistle, I have it all figured out. The brakes. It's just one giant experience of sound and rhythm. And I have songs in my mind, all the time. All the time. But it seems I'm never home. I'm always on the train. So I play songs I've heard in my head, along with the rhythms of the train."

I directed Richard back to the present and then asked him to move to a life in which he played a musical instrument, if such a life was experienced.

Richard: "I'm on a stage playing a violin in Europe. I'm very good. I'm a child, a boy of ten, I'm dressed in a little . . . like a tuxedo, and I'm performing on a stage in a very big place."

I direct him to move forward many years to see if he continues this musical pursuit.

Richard: "I'm conducting an orchestra. I'm very serious about it. The musicians are careful not to disappoint me. We're playing in a big concert hall. We're on a tour, traveling from place to place. All I have are tuxedos in my luggage."

Returning Richard to the present once again, I asked him to further explore his writing lineage. "We explored a lifetime in which you worked on a newspaper and taught English—ideal preparation for your current life as a writer. But is there more? Are there other incarnations that set the stage for the high level of writing success you experience today? If so, on the count of three, new impressions will come in. One, two, three."

Richard: "I run a company that makes expensive pens. Beautiful pens, the best in the world. And I sit at my desk working on my memoirs. Memoirs . . . but there is not that much to say about my pen company. My memoirs would not be very interesting. But I sit and write about people I've known and places I've been."

We established that he lived in Baltimore, before I moved him forward in time and asked, "Are any of your writings published?"

Richard: "I published them. I gave them to my friends. The book is titled *From the Hand*. Everything is just right. And I give it to people. Four hundred sixty-one pages. It is a long book, and it took me a very long time."

"Are you encouraged to write more?"

Richard: "No, I said everything I wanted to say."

"Is the book distributed to bookstores?"

Richard: "I only give the book as a gift. And I give them a pen from my pen company."

At this point, Richard had been in trance for an hour, so I directed him to return to the present and awaken, remembering everything he had experienced in regression.

After awakening, Richard said he had known that Jeanine in the Connecticut lifetime is Diana in this life. She smiled upon hearing this, and I asked her if she were willing to experience past-life regression to explore this on her own. She agreed.

Before sharing Diana's experience in regression, I will share what Tara had to say about Richard's astrological chart.

His Sun is in Libra, Moon in Capricorn, with a Scorpio Rising. In the past life most influencing his present life, I see that Richard returned to be with a father figure. In this important past life, he was wrenched away from his father. There was mutual fulfillment and status of some kind, but that life lacked time with close-knit family.

Richard's Rising shows a profound and studious mind. Mercury in the First House of self, personality, and self-image says he acts on his communication skills. The occult is here and glamour, honor, poetic and artistic ability. It also shows he makes money with his communication skills. Very deep thinking. His work generates popularity.

A lot of changes are indicated and life adjustments have resulted. Some of these changes have been traumatic, but somehow even the undesirable experiences turn into good luck, because his part of fortune sits there. He will always get where he needs to go.

His fascination aspects are on his speaking ability and how he connects to his emotions. People are fascinated by him. Success and high ambition, plus keen perception again. I read sudden luck in creative projects and sudden luck in romance. Having notoriety and being oddly extravagant in his career serve his career.

In regard to others in his life, there will be subtle and hidden changes on his part and on the part of others. When there are obstructions, when he is held back, it is usually for his benefit. The Universe is protecting and guiding him. He set this up to hold himself back, so it's a good thing.

Looking at Richard's uniqueness, I see that maintaining harmony doesn't always serve him. To be too harmonious may be riding the dragon's tail—a matter of generating unnecessary complications and conflicts. Not that he isn't charitable and responsible. But he needs to keep in mind that it is one thing to give, but another to be taken advantage of.

A happy life is here for the taking. Pluto in the Tenth House of profession and ambitions says his work was destined to be in the public. This brings his identity into play. Mental competence sits here, as well as having others work for him—probably his agent, manager, and the film companies that produce what he writes. Music and art appreciation, knowledge of human nature, and strong passions are indicated. He is assertive and disciplined and his jet fuel sits in the house of career.

Prophetic instincts are always in play behind the scenes. The most intense aspects in Richard's chart relate to his communication skills, luck, faith, trust in friends, and money—treasure and profit. He set this life up well.

In summary: Richard's astrological chart accurately reflects his life. The past-life ties are rich examples of how an incarnation evolves into another life. The life with Diana as Jeanine surely set the stage for their present union and his writing career as well. The man who owned a pen company and wrote his memoirs must have thirsted for wider readership. Lifetimes as a child violin prodigy and as a railroad engineer enchanted by the rhythms of the train were ideal prerequisite incarnations for his drumming career today.

Tara's astrological reading claimed Richard also incarnated to be with a father figure. His father, Richard Matheson Sr., is a successful screenwriter and author of novels that have been made into movies, such as *Somewhere in Time* and *What Dreams May Come*. Father and son often work together on film projects. Richard's book *Created By* carries this dedication: "For my father, Richard. My remarkable teacher and friend. My brilliant inspiration. I love you."

Following Richard's regression, we all talked about the experience over a cup of coffee. Initially, Diana seemed a little apprehensive about going through the past-life process, but Richard assured her that impressions would simply flow into her mind. The secret was to trust and be willing to verbalize what you were seeing or feeling.

I hypnotized Diana and directed her to go back to the shared lifetime Richard had described. The exploration would begin when they met in the library, if indeed this were valid. She was soon deep in an altered state of consciousness and when she stepped out of the time tunnel, I asked, "What do you perceive?"

Diana: "I know something of him. His name is John . . . and he's been frightened and alone for most of his life. He tries to hide it. He seems sweet."

"Tell me about yourself. Step outside of yourself and tell me what you look like, how old you are, and what you're wearing?"

Diana: "I'm fourteen. My short hair is dark brown. My dress is kind of plain, maybe melon-colored and soft. It goes straight from the neck to below the waist, and there's a skirt beneath that."

We established that John and Jeanine bonded because they both shared an "aloneness." I directed her to go to the day of their wedding.

Diana: "This comes to me as June 12th. There are no people there. He doesn't really have people, and I don't have people. I see a quiet, small stone church that we just decided to go to on a Sunday afternoon. One other person from the church is there. It doesn't matter to us."

"Let's move forward to an important event in your life, Jeanine."

Diana: "There has always been trouble having babies. We've tried, but it doesn't seem to happen. It was hurtful."

"Are you experiencing the disappointment?"

Diana: "Yes. It's always quiet afterward."

"How many times have you lost a child?"

Diana: "Two times. It's quiet between us, because we don't know why this happens."

I directed her to a time she does give birth.

Diana: "I see a little baby girl. I'm happy and tired. I'm in a hospital. John is happy. He's relieved. He wanted a boy."

"Let's move on to an event you perceive to be important."

Diana: "I feel something about John's grandfather. There was hardship. He came over or was in the war. Polish. His grandfather has passed."

I asked her to tell me about where she and John live.

Diana: "When you walk in, you walk into the kitchen, and there is a table in the middle of the room. From there, you can walk into the living room, and the walls are painted in color. There's a window with lacelike curtains that looks out onto the street. Off to the right is the bedroom."

I directed Diana to the last day of her life in this incarnation as Jeanine. "Tell me what's happening."

Diana: "I'm lying in the bed. Mary is there and a priest. Someone else is bustling about—a neighbor. Mary is grown. She's on the right-hand side of the bed."

"Have you been ill for long?"

Diana: "I think so."

I directed her, without pain and without emotion, to experience the dying process and then speak up and tell me about it. "Can you see the body you just left?"

Diana: "I can look down. It was a broken body. It wasn't a good body."

"What do you feel about being set free?"

Diana: "I'm feeling like home. I've been feeling somewhat disconnected for awhile. So it was just a matter of time."

"You were ready to cross?"

Diana: "Yes. Mary is still sitting by the bed. Other people are moving around. It's almost evening, and I don't think they realize I've crossed over."

I directed Diana to let go of the after-death images, return to the present, and then ascend up into Higher Self. When she had attained a transcended level of consciousness, she said, "I'm in a room with bright, bright, bright light, coming down from above like rays. I sense a presence to my left. It's not a body, but more like a shift or a depression in the light, pushing itself forward. I'm getting the name James. I had a grandfather named James."

"Can the presence provide you with any understanding?"

Diana: "There has to be darkness to see light. This is one of the harder things . . . for souls to chose to be dark. There is no judgment. It's just that it has to be."

"Do you understand this in a larger context?"

Diana: "I do. He was scaring me a little. Like he was pushing in and it was making my heart race. He was an 'inevitable.' There are different energy sources and some are inevitable. It's almost like roulette. When you choose to come through again, at certain times, energies will choose to come through with you and they're not always good."

Further questions and answers revealed that Diana feels a dark energy may have followed her into this life and could have been responsible for the abusive childhood she experienced.

"Maybe we can find value in exploring the abuse. Have you had ties with your father in other lifetimes? Here in Higher Mind, all knowledge is right at your mental fingertips. Simply trust what comes in."

Diana: "Oh . . . it was my grandfather who set this into motion. He was my child in another time, and we had problems."

"You did not get along?"

Diana: "To put it mildly."

"If you were cruel to him, karma was incurred. The abuse you experienced in this life may have been karmic balancing. We've all been victims, and we've all been the perpetrators of human suffering. But the important thing, Diana, is the letting go—the forgiving of yourself, your grandfather, your father, and everyone else involved. Is this something you can do? Can you forgive yourself and forgive them?"

Diana: "Yes, because I know it was done before, to me."

We talked about forgiveness without the need of justification. Diana assured me she was ready to release this dark cycle of cause and effect. There are different possibilities as to what was going on. The dark essence Diana perceived as James may be her grandfather from this life who died and remains earthbound for many reasons, including anger over Diana's relationship with him as a child in a past life. He might have played a part in manifesting Diana's childhood abuse in this life or as a malevolent spirit from the other side. What Diana termed "an inevitable" could be the karmic energy following her into a new life. Since there is no way to avoid karma, balance is inevitable. I made notes to follow up on this the next time we had a chance to do a hypnosis session.

Next, I asked Diana about the past life most affecting her present life, and I directed her to explore this.

Diana: "I'm a girl with long hair and wearing a white dress. I'm seventeen. I think it's England. There are thatched roofs. Shingles hang in front of the shops."

I moved her forward until something important happened.

Diana: "I'm at a formal party in a big hall. Many people are here. I'm here with my family."

"What is your age at this time?"

Diana: "It is past my 'coming out.'" She pauses, says, "Eighteen. I wanted to come to the party because I know there is someone I am supposed to meet."

I moved her to the meeting.

Diana: "A soldier. He has a sash and medals and dark hair. A blue coat and white trousers. I dance with him."

I moved her ahead to explore the outcome of this relationship.

Diana: "I have a letter from my husband, Charles. He is gone to war. The letter has been a long time coming."

"Let's move forward to a time when Charles comes home, if he returns."

Diana: "He doesn't come home. He was killed in the war."

I returned Diana to Higher Mind in the present time and asked, "Is Charles in the past life anyone you know in your current life?"

Diana: "Charles is completely Richard."

Before awakening Diana, I asked if there was anything else she wanted to explore.

Diana: "I keep hearing the word 'healing.'"

"What does this mean? Is there something you need to be doing in regard to healing, or does it refer to relationship healing?"

Diana: "From this time forward, my life is healing. A big hurdle has been crossed. But you have to remove your ego-self to heal. You take out the core, step outside of yourself and let yourself be . . . like you do when you cross over. I have to be quiet now and simply allow happiness in."

I counted Diana awake. She held out her arms to Richard and looked as if she were about to cry as they held each other.

A few days later, Tara completed Diana's astrological chart:

> She is a Leo Sun, Aquarius Moon, and Gemini Rising. Diana's parents were very, very intense, and are at intense opposition in her chart. Diana felt imprisoned by her father in this lifetime, but somehow needed to be there for him or for the family. She was in this position longer than she emotionally wanted to be.
>
> She doesn't give herself credit for progressing fast enough. There is a strong good luck aspect relating to Mars and survival instincts. Diana represses herself in ways when it comes to others. She hides a bit. She has also taken care of the family in a recent past life—helped keep everyone together. And that's been her role in this life—keeping people together under circumstances that aren't always desirable. Radical adjustments are indicated. There is a pattern of assertion and cooperation, a bit of a dual nature that probably fits her well due to the Gemini Rising.
>
> She loves learning, higher knowledge, psychology—an avid learner. She'll be learning all her life. She'll always say the right

things and be balanced in how she says them. An unusual sense of humor, an unusual home life, and an usual love life are indicated. She is also attracted to unusual people. At the same time, she desires security and to explore her creativity. She would do best in a future-oriented artistic career. If she puts her creative foot forward, she will be popular and her business will take off.

Other people are her greatest source of . . . mud. They bring her the greatest gifts or they bring her confusion. At the same time she is loved and fulfilled by other people if she allows them into her life.

The most intense aspect in her chart is at 21-degrees Libra, and Richard's Sun is at 20-degrees Libra. This means their coming together would be cathartic and certainly one of the most important experiences in this life. This aspect creates a binding fascination between the two of them—a wonderful connection.

In summary: I was unfamiliar with what Diana described as "an inevitable," but it is not unusual to encounter new terminology in doing this kind of research. Even some of Abenda's words in the first chapter were unknown to me, and I have been studying this subject all my adult life.

Some of my most extensively researched case histories have illustrated how an angry entity can follow you into death, and then when you reincarnate it can remain on the Other Side as an earthbound force dedicated to working against you. Diana's grandfather is a concern, for this may be what she has experienced. But if Diana can truly forgive herself and forgive him for any and all past wrongs, she can end the association, and her grandfather will have to find someone else with a karmic configuration matching his own need of learning. Eventually he will find there is no value in hating.

In addition to the shared past life Richard and Diana initially explored, she talked of Richard as Charles, her husband, a soldier who never returned. In my experience, when lovers have been separated by death or circumstances beyond their control, they both continue to experience a soul longing that can last for centuries—until they are reunited once again. When they do come together in another life, there is always an intensity to the meeting. This might be instant attraction, confusion, or even fear, which is a subconscious reflection of the pain caused by the past-life parting. I have found that many sexual affairs result from such reuniting.

For a final look at Richard and Diana, Tara ran a composite astrological chart that showed their life together:

> The past life most affecting their present life shows a daughter and very unusual artistic ways. There was great harmony between them and they both shared a love of books, writing, or art. They were a family, and today Diana definitely comes to Richard from a family lineage.
>
> This composite shows their relationship was a surprise. They both love to talk to each other, and love each other's minds. They initially had to do some reorienting for the relationship to work. In the area of material values and possessions, there are considerations about security. They are passionate together and love to make each other feel secure.
>
> Romance is huge in this chart, as are luck and harmony. They've gone through their tests and now they're on "go." The union was destined to be—their soul goal. The most intense aspect in this composite chart is Richard and Diana's sex drive and the communication between the two of them.

In summary: This is an accurate three-paragraph synopsis of Richard and Diana's relationship. In this life, neither has had any desire for children, which may or may not relate to the past-life pain and disappointments they experienced when she failed to carry the first two pregnancies full term. "It was hurtful. It's always quiet afterwards," Diana said sadly. There are some parallels here to the chapter on Shauna and Bert and their desire to experience a lifetime they could devote to each other without distractions.

It seems to me Richard and Diana are playing out their karmic roles the way they wrote them, and they are evolving in the process. In addition to her other work, Diana has been writing and providing Richard with conceptual and editorial assistance on some major television projects. She is also currently taking art classes, which will generate a successful outcome, according to Tara's astrological take.

Richard continues to stretch as a writer and a musician, and he recently told me he is opening the door once again to the kind of psychic investigation he was involved with in college.

11

Reverend Fatima Abate

"Love nothing but that which comes to you woven in the pattern of your destiny. For what could more aptly fit your needs?"
—Marcus Aurelius Antoninus, Roman emperor

"You guys have to come with me to one of Fatima's group healing sessions," said Tiffany Silver, one of Tara's girlfriends. Tara and I had attended a concert by spiritual singer-songwriter David Newman at a yoga center in Topanga Canyon. We were saying our goodbyes to friends in the parking lot when Tiffany brought this up.

"I've never heard of Fatima," I said.

"She doesn't advertise," Tiffany said. "She's from Sao Paulo, Brazil, and she founded The Messengers of Light—a healing group that uses her techniques. Two or three months a year, she comes here to teach and heal."

We hear about many practitioners in the healing and New Age

field, and there is no way to keep up with all of them. I shrugged my shoulders.

"People come from all over the world to see her." Tiffany knew she wasn't getting through to me, so she focused on Tara.

Two weeks later, Tara and Tiffany attended a Wednesday evening Messengers of Light group-healing session in West Los Angeles limited to 30 people.

My wife returned from the three-hour session saying, "Fatima set off my Kundalini. I've never experienced anything like this in my life." She held one hand to her forehead, the other to her tailbone. "The gathering takes place in a Masonic Lodge. We sat on three sides of a large room beneath a huge Masonic pentacle on the ceiling. In the middle are eight massage tables. The lights are low and soothing music is playing. You meditate in your chair until you're picked to lie upon a massage table. First, one of the helpers worked on me, then Fatima began recycling my energy for several minutes. When she touched me, it felt as if she activated a motor in my back, releasing energy discs up my spine and into my head. I felt euphoric."

As metaphysically aware as Tara is, she had never studied Kundalini—a Sanskrit term for the uncoiling of power up the spine. As Kundalini ascends through the chakras, it activates these energy centers and enhances psychic powers appropriate to the centers affected. This is said to be a derivative of one of the elemental forces of Nature, and the release is usually the result of long-term yoga practice and/or occult study.

"What's with the water?" I asked, motioning to two plastic bottles of Arrowhead Spring Water with Tara's name upon them. "Fatima energized the water. I'll drink a little a day."

The second time Tara attended a Wednesday night session with Fatima, she claimed to feel Fatima's energy the moment the healer entered the room, which set off Tara's Kundalini again. When it was my wife's turn on the table, she said, "I grasped the table, because I felt like I was going to levitate or leave my body." The next day Tara said it felt as if her spine were several inches wide.

My wife was so impressed with Fatima that she booked a private one-hour appointment for herself and one for our son, Hunter. Soon after, she learned that a new video project would require her to be out of town at the scheduled time. Tara asked me to take her appointment.

"I'm not trying to heal anything," I said.

"She'll balance and align your energies, and if she perceives any blocks, she'll work to release them. Besides, you'll need to take Hunter to his appointment."

At this time, my astrology said, "Fate is in control of your life." The appointment was in the middle of a 10-day period when the Universe would supposedly be manipulating my circumstances. I agreed to take Tara's place.

At the appointed time, Hunter went first. He returned an hour later looking stoned. "Are you okay, buddy?"

"Fine, Dad," he said, melting into a waiting room chair. I looked at him closer. "She is incredible."

I'm used to my son saying such things about techno DJs or a new action movie, but to hear him identify a spiritual healer in such glowing terms was a shock.

When it was my turn, I was led into the healing room where Fatima, an attractive brunette with a warm smile, extended her arms and gave me a full-body hug. I felt engulfed in a surprising surge of energy. Fatima speaks Portuguese softly, and her husband, Rhandy Di Stefano, an American, interprets, a bit louder, right along with her. She meets your eyes, and he looks at her, negating any uncomfortable need on the part of the listener to focus back and forth. I quickly adapted to the rhythm of the verbal exchange.

I was to lie upon the massage table fully clothed. She would work on me, and he would return at the end of the session to share what she wanted to tell me. For the next 45 minutes Fatima did her energy work—sometimes touching my body, sometimes twirling hands above bodily areas. I assumed she was recycling my energy—drawing out unbalanced energy and replacing it with balanced energy. I soon began to mentally drift and had to fight to maintain consciousness. I had experienced similar sensations during Reiki sessions involving energy manipulation, but this was far more intense. A deep altered state of consciousness resulted in a transcendental feeling of being there, but my experiencing of the process was happening through hazy filters.

When the session ended, Rhandy returned, and Fatima explained the process, talked to me about Hunter, and had complimentary things to say about my energy.

I was impressed.

Before leaving, I asked Fatima if she would be willing to be interviewed for a book I was writing. Rhandy explained that many people wanted to write about his wife, but they had not accepted any such invitations.

A few days later, Rhandy called. After my session, Fatima had told him, "He is the one to write about our work."

Six months later, Fatima and Rhandy returned to Los Angeles. Tara began to attend some of the Wednesday night Messengers of Light sessions with Hunter and Cheyenne. When the children heard that Fatima would be teaching a three-weekend "Quantum Energetic Healing Course," they asked if they could attend. Our daughter, Cheyenne, studies metaphysics and prepares special family meals and rituals for all the Pagan holidays. I understood her wanting to add healing abilities to her growing awareness. But Hunter surprised me. Obviously, his contact with healers had generated an interest in the field.

"The classes are expensive," I said. "Those attending will take it very seriously. Are you willing to spend your own money?" They were.

Tara invited Fatima and Rhandy to our house for dinner and to do an interview and regression session. I greeted our guests at the front door, and Fatima gave me a huge hug—energizing me for the rest of the evening.

Tara and I visited with Fatima and Rhandy in our living room while dinner finished baking. This was supposed to be Fatima's day off, but she had spent it working because, as Rhandy said, "How can you say no to someone in need who has traveled halfway across the country to see you?"

I switched on a hand-held tape recorder and set it on the coffee table between us. Tara mentioned that Hunter and Cheyenne were enjoying the healing course. "Cheyenne tells us one of your trainees came all the way from Japan."

Rhandy laughed. "She came here just for the class, and she has a three-month-old baby, and a baby sitter, so the entourage is also sitting in."

I realized Fatima understood most of what we were saying but did not feel comfortable speaking English. "I can teach anyone to do these techniques," she said. "But many factors interfere and influence the flow of the channeled healing energy: who is doing it, how they connect with spirit, how their own energy is doing, how they take care of their energy on the days when they're not doing the healing work. All of that influences. Sometimes new healers get scared, because they feel it is too much for them to handle. They back away to avoid dealing with so much responsibility. Maybe they feel bad the day after they have done healing work. They think, 'Oh, I pulled this from my client, so now it is my disease.' Because of their belief system, they doubt their ability to recycle the energy—which will happen naturally."

"In regard to becoming a healer, to what degree is it natural ability, as opposed to learning through training?" I asked.

"It's a case-by-case basis," Fatima said. "It depends upon each person's life mission. For me this was decided in the between-lives state. Before this lifetime it was already assigned. This is not the first incarnation I've done healing work. I believe that makes a difference in terms of the quality of what happens. Technically, can any person do it? Yes, any person can be trained, yes."

"But is it their Dharma?" Tara said, getting up to take the meal out of the oven.

Over dinner, we talked about living conditions and working in Brazil. Rhandy said that he would like us to come there to conduct seminars. I told him I would be open to that. "The need for spirituality in Brazil is immense," he said. He explained that the affluent portion of the population spoke English as well as their native language. "They are finding that wealth is not everything, and they are exploring spirituality."

Our meal over, I began to conduct a more formal interview, starting with a question about the beginnings of Fatima's work. She explained that she channeled an entity named "Doctor J," and she described her first meeting with him.

"I was pregnant at the time—my first daughter—and I was alone in my bedroom. I was lying down . . . and then someone walked into the room. A spirit just walked into my room. I wondered, who is this guy? He came to my bed, leaned over, and I was so scared I pulled the bedsheets over my head. Then he called my name and said, 'Let's go, we have a lot of work to do.' I couldn't see anything, but I still heard his voice. 'Let's go, we have a lot of work to do,' he said again.

"Since childhood, I have been able to see spirits. I went to Catholic school and there would be masses every day. I would see the altar full of people. People being treated, people being healed up on the altar. One day I said to a friend sitting beside me, 'Look what's going on up on the altar. Why are those people being treated like that?' And my friend said, 'What people? Who is there? Only the priest is up there.'

"I asked, 'Are you sure there is nobody up there?' She said, 'No, nobody.' So I asked, 'What about yesterday, were there people up there?' She said, 'No, just the priest.' So I asked, 'What about the day before yesterday?' And she said, 'No, just the priest.' And that is when it dawned on me: not everyone could see what I could see. But for me it was just natural. My mom was very religious, a traditional Catholic, so I could not talk to her about seeing spirits. When I told the nuns, they said, 'Go pray and they will go away.' So I prayed and they did not go away.

"When Doctor J showed up in my bedroom, I was about 20 years old. I said, 'What do you want me to do? What do you mean?' He told me, 'We are resuming our mission together.' I said, 'What mission? What are we supposed to do?' He said, 'You're going to be working in hospitals; you will be working with traditional doctors and surgeons, famous surgeons in Brazil. That will be your start.'

"And opportunities started opening up to work with doctors. When a surgeon was preparing to operate, sometimes even with X-rays he did not know exactly where to go in. I would put my hand over the area and pinpoint the place. Also, in some cases after the surgery, people would have a lot of pain. The doctors would call me in and say, 'Put your hand over the painful area and tell us what is going on.' I would tell them exactly what the issue was. The doctors would work on the problem again, and it would disappear."

"So when you began your work in the Sao Paulo hospitals you were just responding to Doctor J's instructions?" I asked.

Fatima nodded in response.

"Did he ever elaborate on his expectations?"

"There was simply an agreement, a soul contract between us made in the between-lives state. I never doubted it. I completely accepted whatever he would say. I had work to do. I am 100 percent sure in my trust for him. When he directs me to do something, there is never any question about if I should do it or not—never.

"Doctor J put me on the healing path in service to traditional medicine, so I had access to hospitals. I could walk in and out of hospitals because I was known and respected for my abilities. In time I went to the biggest hospital in Sao Paulo, and I started working there on a volunteer basis. Often I would just talk to the patients as they went into the emergency room. I put my hands upon them and caressed them and said, 'How are you doing? How are you feeling?' I would just touch them, in a natural way, not as a formal healing technique. And at that moment, I channeled healing. I knew I was not just caressing them. I was removing whatever ailed them.

"In the beginning, Doctor J would tell me to go places. 'Go here. Go there.' And I would say, 'Why am I going to go visit there?' And he would say, 'Just go.' So I would go and say to the people, 'Hi, how are you doing? Let's have some coffee.' And while I was there, maybe I would feel some weird energy in the room, weird energy in the house. I came to understand my body was becoming a magnet for people's negative energies. I would draw in the energy, and when I felt overloaded with the negative energy, I would say, 'Well, gotta go.'

"Then the next day, or maybe a couple of days later, I would get a call from the person I visited and they would say, 'You know, my life was so confused, but the lawsuit I was dealing with was resolved so easily today. I don't know what happened. I feel great.' And I began to understand, 'Oh, that's how energy works.'

"My spiritual mentors were not very explicit about how to do the work. They never said, 'Do this, do that, move like this.' They wanted me to go through the experience—to learn by doing. This was 30 years ago in Brazil. Nobody knew about such things at the time. I was clearing chakras without knowing they were called chakras."

"Does Doctor J appear to have a nationality, even in spirit?" Tara asked.

Rhandy answered, "Oriental. He chose the letter J because it did not mean anything. It was just a letter. He wanted to avoid any identification with a name, so it is just J for J."

"What was your life like when you were not doing the work?" I asked.

"Very social, traditional, high society. No one talked about these kinds of things, so even though I had no support from anyone, I had a comfortable life, which allowed me to experiment as Doctor J instructed. I never charged anyone in the beginning, because I viewed the healing as charity work for people who had no access to other types of treatments. Later I built a center, and for 12 years, every weekend, I had poor people come into the center. With all my heart, I was devoted to this—every single Saturday and Sunday. I took care of the people who could not afford help. I gave them healing, food, and clothing. These people were so poor, they had nothing."

"Did you have helpers?" I asked.

"People began to volunteer. A person here and there. I built the center near my country house in a rural area. That's where the poor people were. The mayor of the town got involved, and my center also became the town social-services center. But the problem was, my ex-husband started to resent it. He did not want this. He no longer wanted to go to the country house where I devoted myself to the people."

"How many children did you have during this time?" Tara asked.

"I had four."

"What did your children think of Mama and her work?" Tara pressed.

"They loved the work. They wanted to receive the healings, too."

We laughed at this because our children and their friends have also always gone to Tara for psychic readings and to obtain advice from Abenda, Tara's spirit guide.

When our conversation returned to clearing the negative energy from people's homes, I asked Fatima if she often dealt with earth-bound spirits who were feeding the negative energy.

"Oh, my God. There are so many entities. I had to expand the healing work to include counseling of the earthbound spirits who were attached to some people. I trained a few assistants to counsel the spirits. For me to counsel the spirits, I had to lower my frequency as much as possible. But there were higher goals, so I would say, 'Okay, I will do it.' So I would lower my frequency, lower, lower, lower, get denser, denser, denser, until I could connect and communicate with the spirit."

"Could you usually talk them out of your client's body?" I asked.

Fatima nodded and said, "The worst was an entity of very low energy, very dense and very dangerous, who wanted to harm a family. The father was a businessman whom the spirit wanted to bankrupt. The man had hundreds of employees, so everyone would have been out on the streets. The entity had caused a lot of damage. So I went to the man's factory. I was walking around, and all of a sudden this weird energy gave me chills. The quality of the energy was terrible. I perceived the entity cussing, and he wanted to kill people, he wanted to destroy."

Rhandy said, "People think they can just tell the spirits, 'Go to the light.' But it doesn't work that way."

I knew that from my own experiences.

Fatima continued, "We worked through many sessions, many sessions, many sessions, where every time I connected with his energy again—I challenged him again. I worked with three assistants, my counselors, who would also talk to him. I would tell them, 'Try this approach, and then try that.' In response, this entity challenged them. To distract us, he would do things like manifest rats in the room.

"But finally we started to obtain some results. The spirit was starting to calm down a little. His frequency didn't feel so slimy, so it was getting a little higher. It took a dozen sessions, over many days, but in the end, the spirit was completely counseled. He converted to the extent he asked for forgiveness. He let go completely. The businessman's life returned to normal."

Rhandy stressed that he feels living people and earthbound entities are sometimes drawn together because, on a soul level, learning will result for all involved.

I agreed. Even this form of entity contact would be karmic.

Then I decided to change the subject. "Fatima, do people come to you for individual sessions primarily for a specific healing, or do they come because they know the value of keeping their energy clear and flowing?"

"For something specific. Some will say, 'I'm here because I want my prosperity.'"

"Really?"

"If someone desires prosperity, they have to be cleared up energetically. If the meridians are blocked, if they're not aligned, nothing flows. There are specific meridians that affect prosperity."

"Wouldn't the blocks be karmic?" I asked. "Blocks force you to learn needed lessons."

"I believe that," Fatima said. "And sometimes people are carrying over something they believed from a previous lifetime. If they're still attached to an old belief system, they will carry the same blockages. Father John[5] says, 'Karma equals a repetition of the same belief.' That's all karma is. If you change the pattern, you get new results. By changing your inner reference as to how you deal with life, then your energy is unblocked. So people come to me for all kinds of reasons, prosperity, relationship problems, and all kinds of health-related problems."

"I've heard some miraculous stories about physical healings you've manifested," I said.

"What people call miracles are natural processes," Fatima said. "We are surprised that people live so unnaturally. Healing is a natural thing. To experience complete energetic flow, complete alignment, complete clarity, while you're going through life's challenges harmoniously— that's natural. What I do with people is bring them back to what is natural—to the energy of their essence, of their soul. The result is healing."

I asked Rhandy and Fatima about a healing conference they had recently participated in. The Northern California event was primarily attended by scientists presenting healing inventions—technological devices and machines.

"The other presenters all wondered why Fatima didn't have a machine," Rhandy said, laughing. "On the second night, when she was scheduled to lead a group-healing session, no one showed up at the starting time. Doctor J told Fatima to start on time. But I asked her, 'Who are we going to heal?' Fatima said she would use the opportunity to work on her assistant's energies."

"Twenty minutes into the healing, over 30 scientists walked in together," Rhandy said. "They had not been able to find the room. But because the healing event was already underway, we did not interrupt the process to start again. As they walked in, the first eight people were immediately brought to the massage tables to be worked on. Having missed the introductory speech, they had no idea what was happening. You could feel a tense energy in the room, as their analytical and linear minds tried to make sense of something nonlinear. But soon, people began experiencing the energy while being worked on. Some started to cry as an emotional response to old personal energies being cleared up."

I smiled at Fatima, who said, "A neurosurgeon from Japan couldn't keep from crying silently while being treated. It is not honorable for a Japanese man to cry in public, so Doctor J told me, out of respect for his cultural background, just to hold him on the table until he regained his composure and could return to his seat. The next morning he told us the tears he cried have been waiting to come out since he was a child."

"The whole energy of the conference shifted the next day," Rhandy said. "All the scientists wanted Fatima to test their machines. They wanted to develop devices that could help people experience what they experienced in the group session. Doctor J told Fatima that some of the machines could achieve powerful results, but they could not provide the love she emanates. Her love spread to everyone attending the conference, influencing their interactions. The conference ended up feeling more like a family gathering."

Over dessert, Rhandy said, "I've been meaning to ask you. I was going over old papers from several seasons back, and I saw your name, Tara Sutphen, and your same phone number in our records."

Tara shook her head. "I had never heard of Fatima or The Messengers of Light before Tiffany talked me into coming to a group session in August."

"It is your phone number," Rhandy said. "There's a note saying referred by Patricia. Who's Patricia?"

Neither Tara or I knew a Patricia. "You have our unlisted number, which we rarely give out," I said, humming the *Twilight Zone* theme.

We had spent hours talking, and Fatima was tired from working all day. We decided it was time to do a past-life regression.

To encourage intimate conversation in our home, we have two living-room couches facing each other over a rectangular coffee table. On a wall a few feet away is a large fireplace, which helped warm the room on this chilly February night. Fatima made herself comfortable on one couch, while Rhandy sat on a chair near her head. He would listen to her and translate over a headset microphone. I work with a microphone, to surround my subject with sound and ensure that I capture all the words on tape. Tara sat beside me on the other couch, notebook in hand, ready to chakra-link to Fatima.

I induced the altered state and directed a visual connection between the two women—heart through crown chakras. When the countdown was complete, I said, "Let's explore how you came to your healing work. We've talked about the soul contract made between incarnations. But let's begin this session by investigating the circumstances leading up to your current life." I directed Fatima to allow her Higher Self to choose the lifetime we would explore, and I counted her through the time tunnel.

"What do you perceive? What are you doing?" I said.

Fatima: "I'm in a room with much light, so many colors, so many people. Everyone is working. Working. Taking care of the wounded ones. All these sick people. So many need to be taken care of." Fatima began expressing anxiety with her body. She covered her closed eyes with her hand, as if it would help avoid internal images. "So many people going in and out."

"Can you tell me where you are? The time or the country?" I said.

She seemed confused by the question, so I asked, "How are you helping the people?"

Further questions generated more anxiety, but I learned she was a male helping men, women, and children—some sick, some wounded. When I asked if they were victims of a battle, bombing, or catastrophe, she said, "All of that. And long-term diseases, sudden diseases. I feel overloaded, but at the same time, I trust in my ability."

"All right, I want to explore how this evolves. Move forward until something changes," I said.

Fatima: "I'm meeting with people who are offering me a new position in a different dimension. And I'm feeling a little scared."

I asked what this new position would entail, and she said, "They're saying it will be desirable for me to do work similar to what I do here, but in a different place. For this to happen, I must change my structure."

"What does that mean?" I asked.

Fatima: "I would maintain my individuality, but in a different appearance, in a different place, with new experiences added to those I have had here."

With this response, I suspected Fatima was not experiencing a past life on Earth. "Are you in spirit at this time?"

Fatima: "Yes. The offer is for me to go to Earth . . . to the physical plain."

"If you accept, will it allow you to evolve faster, because you would be taking on more of a burden?"

Fatima: "I have been told, 'It will expand who you are. Expand your sense of self. You will learn new ways of being.'" Following a lengthy pause, Fatima spoke again, saying, "It is a sense of multiplying who I am."

"You appear anguished. In accepting the offer will you be taking on more than you care to commit to?" I asked.

Fatima: "Yes, there is anguish."

Knowing that Fatima was speaking to me from a position in spirit, I decided to take a new approach. "Is Doctor J willing to come through and talk to us? Maybe he can talk to you, and you can share what he is saying . . . or if he is willing to talk directly to me, that would be ideal. Is he there and willing to communicate?"

"Yes."

"All right, Doctor J, why has Fatima incarnated to heal others? Why is she being asked, in many ways, to sacrifice her own life for others?"

Fatima's voice now became louder, stronger, and she spoke quickly with self-assurance. I assumed that Doctor J was now using Fatima's vocal cords. "To begin, nothing is a sacrifice, for in the world of spirit everything is possible—unlimited. All the particles of oneself represent God. All of the sense of oneself represents God. All the work that is done represents God. This is God activating through oneself. It is God being materialized. It is God creating. It is God doing. It is knowing that things simply get done, things get produced. Life produces itself, always. Life is experience. Life is expanded at every moment, in every gesture, in every smile, in every touch.

"The sense of oneself is being who one is. It is serving humanity. Serving all living beings. Knowing that once you are served, you are also always served by tapping into the inexhaustible source of life. It is being in contact with the principal, and in the principal and in the end at the same time. The end is the eternal cycle in the eternal circular movement of life, of creation, of the sense of being.

"Fatima was sent here along with other beings to develop the multidimensionality of who they are, in order to be more aware of the multidimensionality of every being. She is here because she can be. Just as everyone can be. Everyone can be working toward the same goal, each in their own style—always with a goal of expanding who one is—multiplying who one is. The great challenge is to be able to do this without anxiety, without expectation—simply doing it, and doing it, and doing it. If it hurts, do it. If it gives you pleasure, do it. If it makes you smile, do it. If it makes you cry, do it. Do it, do it, do it, and keep doing it, because at the end, your light is in God."

"Thank you," I said. "Was Fatima chosen because she had obtained a high-vibrational level that would allow her to do this healing work? I can't imagine she was chosen at random."

Doctor J: "Certainly, through her vibrational frequency, certainly through her evolution as the spirit. The spirit is in a state of evolution, and it has gone through many, many different stages and much training. And she has an ability to connect with people on a very uncommon level for the earthly plane. This is needed on the planet. It is the ability to connect on an uncommon level through common movement or common touch. When this contact is established, people's sense of Universal identity is awakened. Much has been done, much growth has occurred, much work has been developed.

"That is why, this lifetime, she was invited to draw upon her experiences and challenged to use her abilities to develop her own senses—the knowledge of who she is, of her potentials. Doing this will awaken more confidence in who she is."

I waited several moments to make sure Doctor J had finished speaking, before asking, "In regard to the people Fatima helps, is it their karma to be helped by her, or have they made some sort of soul decision, which opened the door to her assistance?"

Doctor J: "Everything happens spontaneously. She is a magnet, and all those who need to be aligned, adjusted, or have inadequate negative energies removed are directed toward this magnet. These are people who are on a vibrational frequency receptive to a major healing, and they are able to redirect their own lives into light. Those who are still not of that vibrational frequency will experience the healing on an unconscious level, but the soul is always touched. To experience the healing would be a next step in future evolution. Fatima is just the magnet."

"Will Fatima continue to do this work for a specific period of time, or will she change directions? What can you tell me about Fatima's destiny, Doctor J?"

Doctor J: "She is a spirit in evolution, and she is in the process of shifting directions—finding other means of processing healing in more humanitarian ways. Even greater than now—without having to touch each person individually. The energetic frequency will be amplified so she can shift the healing process as she has in the past. She will be able to talk to larger numbers of people, doing healing processes with a larger number of people."

"I would like to go back to the anxiety Fatima was experiencing at the beginning of this session, while still in spirit. She hesitated to accept the offer, but then embraced the idea of coming to Earth to do healing work. Will you elaborate upon this, so I can better understand this process of being offered the opportunity? Am I correct in understanding that this was an offer, not a directive?"

Doctor J: "She had the option of continuing the work she was doing, or she could come here and do a different practice on Earth. One of the reasons for the offer was to provide her spirit with a more solid foundation of confidence and to diminish that level of anxiety or the hesitation of not fulfilling the duties, which were inadequate residues to her own evolution at the time. Because of the experiences she has had, she was able to overcome this old anxiety and develop her sense of trust and confidence, which places her in a position of being much more fully expanded, much more illuminated. And her guides and friends applaud her accomplishments."

"Can you tell me about Fatima being the male doctor feeling responsible for healing all the people? Where was that taking place?" I asked.

Doctor J: "That was in the hospital where we belong. It is known as the Temple of Healing, and it exists in the spiritual dimension where we work."

"So was this reality or training?"

Doctor J: "These were the people who come to us after they have made the transition from Earth. So this work is always intense."

"So Fatima was helping those who had just died on Earth?"

Doctor J: "All those who cross over to this side are taken care of, are helped to recover and redirected to the communities where their spirits are to reside—centers of recovery. It is very intense work but also very illuminating."

"So by doing this work, your soul is evolving, even in spirit?"

Doctor J: "The movement of the soul is eternal. It does not matter the place. The work continues."

"Has Fatima had any Earth lives, prior to her present incarnation?"

Doctor J: "Certainly. But it has been a long time since she incarnated. A long time. She has worked on any dimension where there was need. Many earthly experiences, with earthly bodies. Very experiential in terms of the material life."

Sitting beside me on the couch, Tara was drawing upon the chakra link connecting her to Fatima. She had been doing considerable automatic writing, and I could see she was writing about some of Fatima's past Earth lives.

"In ending this session, Doctor J, is there any advice you would like to pass on to Fatima?"

Doctor J: "Get ready, for there is more."

Upon awakening Fatima and Tara, I asked Tara to share what she had written.

"I don't know the time of the first past-life impressions, but they were very vivid. Here is what I wrote: Fatima was a blind Chinese woman who helped heal others. Dr. J would bring her into his shop every day. He gave her a life and she energetically hugged others. She is connected to him as she now brings him back into life. He was attacked along a road on his way to deliver a baby. Robbers stole his medications and tools, and they stabbed him. He forgave them as he died. He then went on to help the blind woman from spirit, bringing many people to her side.

"Africa, 1243. Priestess of a shaman. Many come for healing, and she loves this life. She is well respected.

"Copenhagen, 1430, a male incarnation as a scientist trying to do some surgeries. They do not want him to perform these operations, so he is put in a dungeon, where he dies.

"Poland, 1530. A male doctor treating an epidemic of measles. Everyone is sick. He is losing people left and right, especially the elderly and children. He feels terrible for the families. They are horrified and so afraid, so heartbroken.

"Next, Bavaria, 1734. A female incarnation, this time as a hospital nurse. You cannot imagine the loss. There are adults and children from all walks of life. It is putrid. She is overwhelmed again.

"Dr. J has been a priest with Fatima on Atlantis. They were very close. They lectured together and held each other in high regard. There was a pact made in the highest temple. They would always call upon each other to help in time of need, in any form of life and being."

Tara also perceived that Fatima was once an Egyptian ruler who was murdered by his brother, freeing him from a burdensome incarnation. She saw Fatima and Rhandy together as priests in China, Japan, Australia, and the Pacific Islands. "Much, much love," she wrote.

According to Tara, many who come to Fatima today come to her from past lives, although "there is usually no long-term contact with clients beyond their sessions."

Tara finished, "Fatima's many other lifetimes prepared her for this incarnation. She decided to assist mankind throughout this time of faster vibration—helping those in need of mental, physical, and spiritual healing. The world will change and her gifts will live on to give hope and peace."

A few days after our evening with Fatima and Rhandy, Tara finalized Fatima's astrological chart:

Fatima is a Leo Sun and Cancer Moon with a Cancer Rising. This is a wonderful, inspiring chart that reflects Fatima's career and Dharma. Pluto in her first house with her Sun gives her great power of artistic expression and provides her with the extra jet fuel to put her into a place of action. Artistic expression comes up again and again, and in her case probably manifests through her hands as an ability to manipulate energy.

She is pushed forward into groups. Increases in benefits and surprises are indicated. Radical adjustment was required to bring her to the place she is today. And she is driven to make everything right in her life. Her love of family is very strong—her whole family—her lineage. They love and appreciate her as well. Karma is somehow related here.

Fatima was destined to speak. It says over and over throughout this chart that she has intelligence, skill, and speaking ability. She was destined to do exactly what she is doing in this life—helping people resolve their deepest, darkest aspects. She draws upon a high degree of psychic ability for guidance. Divine guidance is also indicated.

I perceived good luck in publishing and higher learning aspects. On the Midheaven, which is service to mankind, she has honor, eminence, and artistic ability. She is surrounded by large numbers of people, and exile is a factor. I thought that was interesting. She is supposed to be a person of the world who leaves home to go out to a lot of people. She does, however, love a steady home base.

Protection from the Other Side is a powerful force in this chart. She has a spirited, brave, courageous nature, and it takes courage to be different—to place yourself in the midst of those who want so much from you. In exploring her most intense aspects, I find fame, recognition, and transformation.

Tara also explored Rhandy's astrological configurations.

He is Aquarius Sun and Scorpio Moon with a Libra Rising. And according to this chart, he definitely came in to be supportive of Fatima. They are tied together very heavily on his descendent, which indicates his relationships with other people. Her marriage aspects sit there. So right away, I see their marriage.

Rhandy's interests in psychology and the mysteries of life are indicated over and over. His security in this life will come through religion, beneficence, mystery, and magic. I see much good fortune and happiness. He is headstrong and broad-minded, and loves anything to do with deep thinking. And he will always be moving around, as is reflected in Fatima's chart, but they both love their home—love being home, being together.

Creativity in Rhandy's chart is expressed in his communication skills. Success and good luck are indicated in writing and publishing. He has the energy and karma for writing if he decided to move in this direction. Popularity is also indicated—harmony with groups. Public honor. His most intense aspect is in regard to service and marriage.

I asked Tara to also explore Fatima and Rhandy's composite astrological chart to provide an even clearer picture of their shared soul contract.

They are here to help each other to become all they can be. Their composite chart tells me they have been together in many lifetimes, but could not marry in their last life. While doing their chart, I perceived visions. In a Yugoslavia lifetime they loved each other very much and were married and in a public position. But the country opposed their beliefs, resulting in the army capturing and killing them both. I also received a vision of Rhandy being a priest in a small Italian town, wishing he could marry

Fatima. He loved her holiness and beauty and regretted locking himself up in a priest's life.

They have an "in-synch" Sun, Moon, and Rising—very together here, which comes into play with Pluto. This propels them down the proper path. Even when the path appears dark, when they go with their intuition, the path becomes clear on a karmic level.

They can be temperamental with each other but are courteous, refined, and lovable. It is just to reorient. With so many Earth signs together, they're really into pleasing each other and being of the Earth. Their shared friendship is strongly indicated. Their speaking ability together is in a place of honor.

Their most intense aspect in the composite chart is their romance together—their accord and harmony. It also hits the Sun and Mars, their good luck aspects and emotional nature. This is a relationship in which they were absolutely born again to be together. No way around it. With Rhandy's soul goal and Fatima's Dharma to mankind, they could not have not come together. These are incredible aspects.

In summary: Hunter and Cheyenne completed Fatima's course and were certified as Quantum Energetic Healers. A few days later, Rhandy called Tara to say he and Fatima were amazed by Hunter's natural ability to work with energy. When Tara attended a Wednesday night healing session in March 2004, Fatima took her aside to say how proud she was of Hunter. "It is his destiny to be a healer in this life," she said. She went on to explain that our son was in direct contact with the Temple of Healing and Doctor J.

Tara reminded me that Don Schnell (chapter 8) had also said Hunter was destined to be a healer. Tara and I believe Hunter's alopecia areata condition may have been destined to put him in contact with healers who would guide him toward this path.

Fatima and Patti Conklin (chapter 9) were born to be healers, and they shared some similar experiences before beginning to fulfill their destiny. As children, they each had the ability to see beyond the veil. When they got older, both women were contacted by spirit and verbally directed. Today, they work in different ways but obtain similar results.

Souls with the kind of power Fatima and Patti demonstrate have always experienced prerequisite lifetimes working in the same or a similar field. They come back lifetime after lifetime, honing their skills in each incarnation. And while they appear bigger than life because of what they do to help elevate human suffering, they are subject to the same earthly concerns as everyone else. No matter how advanced a soul may be, upon incarnating on Earth, when they act with intent, they incur karma. They must also confront the limits of a physical body and wrestle with the emotional lessons to be learned through relationships.

Why does Fatima converse with Doctor J, while Patti talks with Father, Tara communicates with Abenda, and Katherine Brooks and Donald Schnell have a direct line to Babaji? I don't know why Earth/spirit connections take so many different forms, but it may have to do with the different paths of service each individual has taken to help resolve suffering. Fatima and Patti alleviate pain and disease. Tara's Abenda communications soothe mental suffering by guiding readers to understand their karma. I assume Katherine will make films to assist her audience's understanding of their earthly journey, and Donald, as a swami, is primarily guiding people to experience better lives.

Although the above Earth/spirit connections evolved naturally, I know of many situations in which an individual has set out to establish an ongoing contact with a soul in spirit—maybe their spirit guide, maybe a teacher—sometimes with a deceased relative or friend. Anyone who is clear on their intent and willing to work at developing such a channel of communication can do so.

1 2

Dick Sutphen's Parallel Life[6]

"Man may his fate foresee, but not prevent."
—John Webster, English playwright

Up until now, we have been exploring reincarnation as it is classically understood. There is, however, another dimension to this subject called simultaneous-multiple incarnation—parallel lives, another aspect of the soul agreements we make before incarnating on Earth.

In my book *You Were Born Again to Be Together*, I talked about my introduction to the concept of parallel lives. The book was published in April 1976, and in the fall of 1976, Jane Roberts's book of Seth channeling, *Psychic Politics*, was published. I did not see Jane's manuscript and she did not see mine, but we wrote about the same thing.

I called them parallel lives; Seth called them separate selves. Seth said, "You can live more than one life in one time." Also, "If you could think of a multidimensional body existing at one time in different realities, and appearing differently within those realities, then you could get a glimpse of what is involved. You do not experience your century simply from one separate vantage point."

In this book, I will not go into the technical aspects as to how parallel lives work, but the idea is that you are currently sharing a direct connection with one, two, or three other people—extensions of your soul or oversoul. I have conducted parallel life transference sessions with hundreds of people in seminars, and no one has ever come up with more than three.

Unless parallel lives are a reality, logically reincarnation does not work, for there are nearly as many people now living on the Earth as the sum total of all who have ever lived. So there would not be enough past lives to go around. Those who are doing the historical counting are not taking into consideration lost civilizations such as Lemuria and Atlantis, but that is not important. The thousands of people I have regressed have experienced numerous past lives within recorded history. If they are representative of the rest of humanity, which I feel they are, then numerically reincarnation doesn't work.

But if you factor in parallels, there are only a fraction the number of people on Earth there appear to be. Take yourself as an example. You are you, but at the same time, you may also be a young boy in Vietnam, and an old woman in Mexico, and a middle-aged male in England. You all share the same soul lineage and are spiritually connected. You may also be influencing one another, although you don't realize this on a conscious level. Over the course of your life, a parallel self may die, or a new parallel self may be born. Think of the process as an ever-evolving process of explorations of potential.

I realize this is a difficult concept to accept. At least it was for me, until I spent a lot of time and energy researching one of my own parallel lives as a man named Ed Morrell, who lived in California at the turn of the century. In reading my story, you will learn how your own parallels can exert a powerful influence upon your current life.

In 1975, I was living in the mountains above Prescott, Arizona, and had just finished writing *You Were Born Again to Be Together*. In preparation for my next book, I often interviewed David Chethlahe Paladin in his studio. David was a Navajo shaman who was also a highly acclaimed fine artist. He had the ability to verbally channel, to allow discarnate entities to speak through him. While he was channeling, David's whole demeanor would change and the pupils of his eyes would dilate to the point of becoming solid black.

Wassily Kandinsky, the Russian artist who died in 1944, was the primary identity who communicated through David. During one of these sessions, Kandinsky spoke about a personal friend of David's and how their present relationship reflected previous friendships in other historic periods. In an attempt to clarify a point, I mentioned the name of a close friend. "Can you tell me of other lives he and I have shared?" I asked.

"Visualize him in your mind for a moment," Kandinsky replied in his thick Russian-accented English. "Ah, yes, the two of you have been together several times." Kandy went on to explain details of a couple lifetimes. They made sense and tended to explain some underlying aspects of our friendship. Then he continued: "From your perspective, you might not agree, but you also owe him a great deal. He was one of those who was responsible for your being sent to prison, but because of this, you met Jack London, and it had a strong influence on your becoming a writer."

I questioned Kandy no more about it at the time, but later asked a writer friend if London had ever been in prison. "Once for lobster poaching and another time for vagrancy," he said. That was the extent of my follow-up. It was an interesting bit of information, but only one of hundreds of interesting things I was investigating at the time. As a young boy I had read many of London's outdoor books, but I didn't identify with the man beyond that. The information was more or less forgotten for almost a year, until I was sitting on the front porch of my home, visiting with Richard Bach, author of *Jonathan Livingston Seagull* and *Illusions*. "By the way, Dick, have you ever read a book of Jack London's called *The Star Rover?* It's about reincarnation and astral projection . . . about a man in prison."

"Why are you asking?" I said.

"I don't know," he said. "It just came in. You really should read it, though. It's quite hard to find because it was printed shortly after the turn of the century and was never one of London's more popular books. I have a copy, and if you can't find one, I could photocopy it for you."

A month later, while having Sunday brunch with David Paladin and his wife, Lyndia, I recalled Bach's words about Jack London's book. Addressing myself to David, I asked, "Kandy, you told me something about a year ago that I'd like to ask more about, if you don't mind?"

David's eyes changed—the pupils dilated and an alien intensity became quite obvious. "Of course," replied the familiar voice of my Russian friend.

"Well, you told me I was in prison, and through this I met Jack London and it influenced my writing career."

"Remember, there is no time, so although you may think of it as your last life, it is still transpiring. Yes, you were in prison, but they couldn't keep you there . . . you kept astral-projecting out. They could imprison your body, but not your mind or spirit. You will soon come to know much more of this."

The following month, Joanne Ordean, a friend in Los Angeles, located a copy of *The Star Rover* for me. Once I started reading it, I could not put it down. London narrated the story of Darrell Standing, a fictionalized account of the prison life and adventures of Ed Morrell. The book began with an imprisoned Standing awaiting execution, but told nothing of why he was in prison. It described the hideous agony of "the jacket," a device to torture inmates in solitary confinement, and how Standing developed self-hypnosis and astral-projection as techniques to survive confinement periods with "the jacket." While out of his physical body, he could travel anywhere in the world; he also found that he could go backward in time and relive his own past lives.

The next step in unraveling the mystery was library research. I found that nine years after the publication of Jack London's book, Ed Morrell wrote the true story of his experiences in his own volume titled *The 25th Man*. The search was now on in earnest, but I could not find the book. It was not listed in any of the 1924 book releases or *Books in Print* catalogs. The owner of an antique bookstore who made his living finding out-of-print books told me, "I think it was self-published, so there is no knowing how many copies were actually printed. It is probably impossible to find."

Although this was a dead end, I had learned that Morrell was involved in metaphysics, hypnosis, writing, and self-publishing—my primary interests and occupation—all of which had come easily to me. It almost appeared that I was an extension of Ed Morrell. I had been interested and involved in metaphysics for years. Upon first receiving instructions in hypnosis, I knew it and was quickly creating techniques to accomplish things my teachers said were impossible. My own publishing company was successfully publishing books for the professional art and advertising market.

Was I the reincarnation of Ed Morrell?

The Los Angeles Public Library listed *The 25th Man* in their files, but were unable to locate the book. *You Were Born Again to Be Together* had been published by Simon & Schuster Pocket Books and I was to go on a multicity seminar tour in support of the book. I forgot about my search for Morrell's book for several weeks. Upon returning home in November 1976, I found among my mail a box from Joanne. Inside, carefully packed in several inches of foam, was a perfect copy of *The 25th Man,* accompanied by a short note: "Herein find one early Christmas present. We located it through a book hunter in New York. Much love, Joanne."

Before my suitcases were unpacked, I had curled up by the fireplace and begun to read.

In the preface, Morrell described how, in 1912, he related his dungeon experiences to Jack London, "Particularly those vivid wanderings in 'the little death' while undergoing torture in the jacket in the dungeon of San Quentin." The author goes on to explain: "I desire to state emphatically that the experiences of mind projection (astral projection) in 'the little death' were very real to me, because I not only projected my mind through the power of self-hypnosis out of the dungeon and into the big, living, moving world of today, influencing the lives of some who were destined to play a great part in my future life, but also I explored time through the ages, reliving lives that I had lived just as surely as I live the present life. More, I was privileged in the dungeon to understand many strange complexities of my checkered career and the purpose for which I been marked for suffering."

To my surprise, the book turned out to be a true Western adventure and prison horror story. Morrell was the youngest and 25th member of a band of settlers who turned outlaws over a land dispute with the railroad. The story takes place in the San Joaquin Valley and the Sierra Nevada Mountains, and is recorded as part of the history of California.

There were many affinities between the information in the book and my current life. As long as I could remember, I had had dreams of hiding in the mountains with another man. I was holding an old Winchester rifle and we were watching men far below tracking us through the mountains—the exact situation in which Morrell found himself on many occasions.

For years before I knew anything about Ed Morrell, an 1894 saddle-ring Winchester carbine was mounted on pegs above my fireplace. Upon finding it in an Arizona antique shop, I had to have it. Just holding this rifle had always given me a sense of peace and security I did not understand, until I learned it was the same model that Morrell used.

In his book *We Immortals*, Alan Weisman reports the first of many past-life hypnotic regressions that I experienced with different hypnotists. In a deep trance, I relived many of the experiences that Morrell wrote about and many more that were not included in the book. Most of the then-unknown experiences I was later able to verify. As an interesting example, in the session with hypnotist Jean Perry in 1977 in which I was hypnotically reliving Ed Morrell's life, I was asked, "Do you write?"

I responded, "I've been trying to write, but I don't know how."

I did not understand at the time, for obviously Morrell wrote *The 25th Man*. It was years later I uncovered the fact that, when the book's copyright needed to be renewed, Morrell's wife proved she had actually authored the book under his name because Morrell was unable to write.

In March 1981, I decided to take a few weeks to formally investigate the Ed Morrell lifetime. The search began at the Visalia, California, public library. Arriving before the library was open, I used the time to walk through the streets of the small town. I had no feeling of familiarity, but most of the construction was new.

Walking back in the general direction of the library, I froze. Not only was there a feeling of familiarity, it was a very uncomfortable familiarity. The sign etched in marble over the door read: "The Tulare County Jail." The jail was a two-story brick building, now standing empty, the broken windows exposing rows of jail cells. Closer inspection, especially of the second floor cells, made my skin crawl.

"This is the door they took us out to avoid the lynch mob," I said to myself almost without thinking. The jail is a large building with many doors, yet records I was soon to examine proved the accuracy of the statement.

For the next few days I checked the microfilm records of several newspapers and searched through the special California history collections in libraries as well as Fresno State University. One library assistant would send me to another; I ran back and forth between some of the towns, each time finding a little more information. Often one fact would create a bigger puzzle, yet it usually led down the line to increased awareness of exactly what had transpired. Finally, at the end of the week, my briefcase was filled with a three-inch stack of photocopied records and newspaper stories, as well as many rolls of photographic film.

After going over the material and using hypnotic investigation techniques, I felt I had a more accurate picture of what transpired during 1893 and 1894 than had been previously reported by anyone, including Ed Morrell's own book, *The 25th Man*. There are sections in the book that never felt quite right; I believe that Morrell left out some important information to cast himself in a better light, and that portions of the book were embellished to create more sympathy for his cause: prison reform. Yet basically it was all true and, for adventure, the story rivals anything in the history of the American West.

As new details of Morrell's life began to surface, I was disturbed. I did not want to have been this man. The concept of a Western "outlaw" is quite romantic, yet the contemporary version of that word is "criminal." But the more I uncovered, the more obvious it became that he had learned from his mistakes.

After his release from prison, Morrell successfully initiated much-needed prison reform in many states. He is considered the father of the honor system and, due to his success, was called before the U.S. Congress to speak. His wife collected countless letters and articles which testify that he was much admired by many great men: governors, judges, statesmen, noted newspapermen, famous American authors and poets, world-renowned psychologists, psychiatrists, and occult authorities.

Edward Brennan (Morrell) was born in 1869 in Pennsylvania. He was working in the coal mines by the age of nine. As a teenager, Morrell ran away from the poverty and squalor of this life to find work in Jersey City. Morrell later stowed away on a cattle boat bound for Europe and, by working his way on various ships, began to travel the world. The fakirs and other mysteries of India sparked his interest in occult potentials. In Australia a wealthy man named Morrell started adoption proceedings, promising to send him to school in England. When the man did not live up to his word, Morrell left, crossing the country on horseback and boarding a steamer in Sydney outbound for San Francisco.

When jailed in Fresno for a misdemeanor, Morrell met Chris Evans of the Evans-Sontag outlaws. Evans's group had been successfully holding up Southern Pacific trains for several years. At the time, the railroad was a predatory corporation that dominated the politics and economic life of the people living in the San Joaquin Valley. After the railroads blatantly cheated hundreds of small farmers and ranchers and unnecessarily killed many in what is known in California history as the "Mussel Slough Massacre," several of these ranchers began to rob the trains in retaliation. For the first time, dynamite was used to blow open the express cars, making the robberies highly successful.

Evans was the subject of a massive manhunt and shootout that went on for months in the San Joaquin Valley and nearby Sierra Nevada Mountains. Many lawmen and bounty hunters died by Evans's hands, yet he was a hero to many people who hated the railroad as much as he did. When Evans was finally captured, one eye was shot out and an arm was so badly wounded that it had to be amputated in jail.

Meanwhile, Morrell had been released from jail and was working as a waiter in Stock's Restaurant. It was his job to take the meals to the prisoners in the Fresno jail where Evans was imprisoned. During this time Morrell met Evans's pretty daughter, Eva, and together they created a plan to help her father escape from jail.

A newspaper reporter named Wallace Smith accused Morrell in his book *The Prodigal Sons* of helping Evans because of hero worship, expounding upon the subject like a Pentecostal preacher.

Back to my 1981 research trip: On the second night of the trip, while sleeping in a motel in Visalia, I sat bolt upright at about 4 A.M., my mind full of a dream I had been experiencing. It became clear to me, through the dream, that Ed Morrell admired Evans a great deal, but it was not hero worship—Evans was a father figure to him. Morrell was subconsciously searching for someone to take his dead father's place, which also explained the adoption situation in Australia. The next day I was able to successfully document that Mary Brennan was widowed when Morrell was very young, validating my dream information.

The local newspapers also offered microfilm records of the Evans jailbreak. Morrell convinced Sheriff Jay Scott that the Southern Pacific train was going to be held up outside of Porterville on December 28, 1893. With the sheriff and his deputies off on a wild goose chase many miles to the south, Morrell delivered two revolvers along with the evening meal. Evans and Morrell, both armed, marched the jailer out the front door of the jail and down Mariposa Street. They soon met the former mayor of Fresno and forced him to accompany them as another hostage, seeking to reach a team and buggy that was tied down the block in front of the Adventist Church. The buggy was stocked with provisions and ammunition.

Morrell ran ahead to untie the team, only to find John D. Morgan, constable of Fresno, and W. M. Wyatt, a former Texas Ranger, visiting at curbside in front of the church, where a chicken dinner was soon to take place. Morrell screamed at them to raise their hands and immediately disarmed Morgan. When Morrell focused his attention on Wyatt, Morgan grabbed him and was quickly shot in the shoulder by Evans, who by now had reached the scene. The shots spooked the horses, who fled down the street, so the outlaws had to run into the night on foot. They soon stole a buggy and quickly made their way to the safety of the Sierra Nevada Mountains. Evans was a mountain man, at home in an environment that was primarily populated by friends who shared his feelings about the railroad. For the next seven weeks these two men made fools of the lawmen, posses, and freelance manhunters who sought their capture.

The newspapers reported one outlaw encounter after another. When three deputies accidentally came across Evans and Morrell at Camp Manzanita, the deputies wished they had not. Morrell described how he chased L. Parker Timmins, who dropped his gun and ran: "I played with him, teased and tried him, drove him over rocks and rough ground and through dense thickets of scratchy manzanita and chaparral. Behind, and all the time just a little above him, I could see every move. Hour after hour he worked his way down the brushy mountainside heading toward the stage station at Dunlap and dodging in and out to avoid the spatter lead which hit all around him." When Morrell was almost out of ammunition, he let the man go.

Often the outlaws were so close to the hunters that they could remain hidden and listen to the hunters' conversations and plans. At Slick Rock, two deputies came upon a mountain home where the outlaws were having dinner with the Robison family. As they approached the house, Morrell stepped out the door, firing his Winchester. One man ran into the trees and did not stop running until he reached the closest town. The other, after losing control of his horse and buggy, eventually managed to get away, accompanied by the sound of the outlaws' laughter.

These reports, plus the fact that newspaper reporters from San Francisco and other cities were always able to find and interview the outlaws, created great pressure upon the law enforcement agencies of California and intensified the hatred of railroad officials, who saw the outlaws as symbols of resistance against the railroad.

For seven weeks lawmen, Southern Pacific gunmen, bounty hunters, and hundreds of volunteers attempted to capture the out- laws, who continued to make fools of their pursuers. It was obvious that they might never be captured. Thus someone decided on a new tactic: to play upon the fact that Evans was known to be an exceptionally affectionate father. The word was passed to Evans that the youngest of his six children was critically ill.

Morrell had traveled to San Francisco and arranged for a ship that would be waiting for them in the Santa Barbara Channel. He argued with Evans against the trip into Visalia to visit the child.

The *Visalia Daily News* on February 19, 1894, read:

> "Captured—Evans and Morrell in the Visalia County Jail."
> They surrendered to Sheriff Kay this morning. Once the outlaws entered Evans' house, they learned his youngest son was fine and the house was surrounded by lawmen. Rather than a gunfight that might have resulted in the children being killed, Evans and Morrell surrendered.

In response to rumors of a lynching, Sheriff Scott arrived from Fresno with two deputies to remove the prisoners to Fresno at once. According to the local newspaper account: "A two-seated surrey drawn by the best team in the livery stable was brought out and driven to the jail by Deputy George Witty. In a few moments, Chris Evans, ornamented with leg shackles, and Ed Morrell with handcuffs were led from the rear north door of the jail." Less than 20 minutes later a lynch mob set off in pursuit of the men but was unable to overtake them.

Evans was quickly sent to Folsom to begin his life sentence, but Morrell remained in the Fresno jail for the next two months while the law and the railroad attempted unsuccessfully to pin a major crime on him. They then offered Morrell a light sentence in return for exposing the other outlaws responsible for the train robberies. When Morrell refused, he was promised the "quickest trial in the history of the state." An angry official warned Morrell, "The sentence will be life in the sunbaked rock quarries of Folsom."

The maximum sentence for holding up the county jail and releasing a prisoner was ten years. With good conduct, Morrell figured he could get out in six.

At the trial, Morrell was charged only with highway robbery for taking Constable Morgan's gun immediately after breaking Evans out of jail. The railroad-controlled jury deliberated for ten minutes and recommended life imprisonment. The judge agreed, sentencing Morrell to life in Folsom.

Many years later, Congressman Denver Church explained that at the time Morrell was sentenced, he was assistant district attorney in Fresno. Church remembered writing in his diary at the time about the "wanton miscarriage of justice" and swore that if he became district attorney, he would reopen the case.

An hour after entering Folsom, Morrell's head was shaved, and he was attired in the wide-band-striped convict uniform and taken directly to the office of the warden. The warden was an ex-railroad detective who had been given his position as a reward for faithful service. The warden let "the San Joaquin train robber" know that he was a special case and invited him to attempt to escape.

Minutes later, Morrell was taken to the outside prison work area, handed a four-pound hammer and point, and instructed to climb a crude ladder to the top of a large boulder. He was told to chisel a hole in the center of the rock all the way down to the middle. If his work slowed or he moved from the spot, he was told Gatling guns would instantly cut him down. "From today on, root hog or die!" laughed the guard. This was an unheard-of spectacle that caused the other prisoners to stop their work and stare in amazement.

For the next four months, Morrell worked from morning to night on top of the boulder. Back in the steel-barred prison house, he received, along with the other inmates, a dinner of "bootleg coffee, dry coarse bread, and a dish of watery, unseasoned beans." As Morrell got to know the other convicts, he learned from them that his life "wasn't worth a nickel." The word was, the power of the Southern Pacific Railroad had singled him out to be "crushed" by the authorities.

The warden's plan was to force Morrell to rebel, providing an excuse to "stretch him on the derrick until he cried for mercy." A guard reported the warden's words: "Don't kill him. I want to drag out a few long, miserable years before we plant him. Keep him on top of that rock for the next year if it takes him that long to dig a hole deep enough so that I can't see him from my office window. By that time I'll have conjured up a new mode of torment for him."

Yet after four months and 11 days on the rock, fate intervened. A visiting state official asked the guard why Morrell was on the rock. When it was explained that the warden had ordered special punishment, the official exploded and ordered that Morrell be given a position as an apprentice learning a useful job. He also demanded that a gang of men immediately split up the boulder so it could not be used for such a purpose again.

Morrell continued his good behavior and began to learn stone cutting, but then the warden instructed the crushing to begin in earnest. At the end of a day's work, a guard accused Morrell of stepping out of line when he had not. He called the guard a "liar." The punishment: 50 hours on the derrick—a sentence normally reserved for convicts who tried to escape. At this time, ten hours on the derrick caused the near-death of any man, and Morrell felt he was being executed. It meant hanging by the wrists from metal handcuffs five hours a day for ten days to complete the 50 hours. The rest of the time was spent on the cold stone floor without a cot or blanket and only enough dry bread and water to keep him alive.

The punishment was accepted without a whimper, his iron will amazing even the hardened guards, but by the seventh day, blood was dripping from Morrell's kidneys, large black circles had formed under his eyes, and his face was ashen white. The prison doctor ordered that he be taken down, not as a gesture of mercy, but to ensure that he would live to experience further torture. Folsom at this time was indifferent to the death of convicts. For three days he lay on the stone floor of his cell recuperating before they again strung him up by the wrists to complete his punishment for three more days. This was the first of many derrick tortures Morrell was to experience during his first year in Folsom. With each experience he became more bitter.

The guards purposely attempted to aggravate him in an attempt to make him rebel. When this failed, they framed him for a prison escape plot. The punishment: being tossed into a cell in which the floor was covered with three inches of chloride of lime and sprinkled with water. Morrell describes the experience in his own words in his book, *The 25th Man:*

I clutched my burning throat with both hands, then reeled and fell to the floor. That only brought me closer to the volcano of fiery death. Struggling frantically, I scratched at the jutting stones of the dungeon trying to pull myself to my feet. I then staggered, groping blindly until I hit the door. I pounded upon it. Cramping pain tore at my bowels. My breath grew hot. It had the intensity of molten lead. My fingers, hands, and arms finally became numb, and paralyzing shocks stunned my brain. Had I been offered a draught of deadly poison in that awful agony, I would have drunk it with gratitude—anything to escape further torture in that lethal chamber of Hell.

The black hole seemed at last to resolve. I felt my position slowly reverse. It now appeared that my head was down and my feet up. Then I started to whirl, and as if obeying some terrific centrifugal force, I was shot off into space.

The door opened and a guard reached in with a long hook and dragged out my limp body. The dungeon tender played the hose upon me. The cooling water stifled the burning fumes and slowly brought me back to life. The whole gruesome deed hardly consumed six minutes in actual time, but I had been dead for ages. Two guards laid hold of my legs and dragged me back to my cell.

What I suffered for the next ten days beggars description. The delicate mucous membrane of my mouth and throat was seared and burnt. My eyebrows and eyelashes were gone. I could not speak above a whisper. Physically I was a wreck, and the day I left the dungeon to report again for work I was a changed man. The iron of hate had branded my heart. Henceforth it would be plot and counter plot. I lived solely for vengeance.

Morrell had now been in Folsom close to two years and he began to focus all of his energy to spearhead a mutiny. He sent a released prisoner to friends in the San Joaquin Valley. The friends hid a large cache of rifles, pistols, and ammunition in the foothills just outside the prison and were ready to cut the phone lines from Folsom to isolate the prison from the outside world.

The elaborate plan was designed to take control of the prison and conduct a court-martial of the warden and brutal guards. "Undoubtedly, their sentence would be death by hanging on the prison gallows." This would be followed by blowing the prison off the face of the Earth.

A few days before the proposed mutiny, a prison stool pigeon betrayed the plot. The warden, rather than reacting with his normal torture punishments, panicked. He turned to state officials and demanded that Morrell and the 24 ringleaders be immediately transferred out of his prison. Two days later, Morrell and the others were in San Quentin.

In response to the transfer, Morrell said, "I lived merely for vengeance and hated the fate that balked my plans for revenge. At any other time but now I would have welcomed the transfer as an act of divine mercy, because San Quentin was not the lockup of the 'Octopus' (railroad), and there I might redeem myself for a life of future usefulness. But now all was changed. I wanted to remain at Folsom. I hungered for the clash. I wanted to hear the sharp crack of the rifles and see men in blue coats and brass buttons fall. If the day went against us, I would have welcomed death."

San Quentin in the late 1800s was infamous as a "man-killing" jail. Again Morrell was marked to be "crushed." This time it was not for his crimes against the railroad, but for his Folsom reputation as the incorrigible leader of insurrections. And if conditions were bad at Folsom, they were far worse at San Quentin. "Folsom had only grumbled, but San Quentin moaned and groaned in terrible, silent ferment. The hospital and the old tubercular ward were filled to capacity and dungeons and punishment cells were jammed full of convicts who had already dared protest. San Quentin was rife with an unspeakable atmosphere of suppressed murder, and only awaited the responsibility of leadership."

Morrell was assigned to work in the prison jute mill and was immediately informed by the captain of the yard, "The first time you bat an eye, you'll think Folsom was paradise by comparison to this place." A few days later, Morrell was accused of "dog-eyeing" a guard and sentenced to 20 days in the dungeon, where he was chained to the wall. When questioned as to why he menaced the guard with his eyes, Morrell refused to answer and was given 35 days in the hole with even fewer rations. It was the first of continual trips to the punishment dungeon. His guard boasted openly that this was a means to avenge the death of a bounty-hunting relative who had been killed by the California outlaws during a chase.

Morrell now decided to take on the task of leadership of the 1,900 convicts residing in San Quentin, and soon organized 100 men to lead a major mutiny in which they took control of the jute mill and held all guards as hostages to draw attention to the hideous prison conditions and seek solutions to their grievances.

The primary demands: the removal of the commissary general and an investigation of the spoiled and inedible food supplies; those connected with their purchase were to be prosecuted for graft; the appointment of a new chief cook by vote of the prisoners; the assignment of stool pigeons and pampered rich prisoners to shifts in the jute mill; the improvement of prisoners' conditions, including a new ruling that a prisoner would be confined to bread and water no longer than ten days, and a prisoner sentenced to dungeon punishment would be supplied a mattress and blankets.

Morrell presented the demands to the warden, who immediately agreed to meet the conditions. This was officially expressed by the captain of the yard to all prisoners. The entire incident occurred peacefully, without physical harm or damage to prison property.

Behind the scenes, the warden and officials quickly planned a double-cross. Morrell was dragged naked from his cell and, with seven of the ringleaders, jammed into a closet-sized cell. Then guards hit them full blast with icy water from fire hoses. The cell, built like a tank, quickly began to fill with water. When the water level reached the taller men's chins, it was shut off. The shorter men had to be supported to avoid drowning. The men, packed like sardines, remained standing throughout the night.

The warden then staged a phony mutiny using prison pets and stool pigeons to quell the inquiries of the press. The state of California heard only about a meaningless insurrection by unreasonable prisoners desiring an easier life.

After nearly a week of punishment, Morrell was sentenced to serve considerable time in solitary confinement. After his release from solitary, a stool pigeon named Sir Harry informed the warden that Morrell had successfully spearheaded a plan to smuggle a cache of guns into the prison and was planning a prison break. Although the charges were unfounded, the officials went into a panic, fearing the consequences if Morrell were able to retrieve the firearms.

The warden ordered 36 days of beatings and tortures in an attempt to extract a confession. A meeting of the board of prison commissioners was called, for the officials were convinced the guns existed inside the walls of San Quentin. Throughout the entire inquiry, Morrell protested that he was innocent. In the end, the board decided there was only one way to make sure the guns did not fall into the outlaws' hands, and the chief inquisitor of the court uttered the sentence: "Solitary confinement for the balance of your life."

The solitary dungeon cell was four and one-half feet wide by eight feet long. Morrell was given a straw tick and two blankets. He was allowed no reading material, and even if he had been, there was not enough light to see the print, for the brightest part of the day allowed only a faint streak of murky light to penetrate a painted window from an outer corridor. Once every 24 hours a scanty meal was slipped under the cell door.

Morrell was afraid the lack of human contact would cause him to lose his mind. He spent most of his time pacing back and forth—three steps and a turn on the fourth. Morrell: "As the months dragged their weary length out into years, my thoughts ran wild, and in the mental battle which ensued, I developed an amazing power of visualization. I began to invent, creating devices mentally, drawing plans upon the walls of my brain, completing each and then starting in on something new, at last experimenting in self-induced hypnosis, daring even to project my mind out and beyond the confines of San Quentin to distant lands and loved ones."

He learned to play checkers in his mind and was extremely successful at training ordinary houseflies, who also lived in his cell. But his primary project was self-hypnosis: "Prone on the floor, I would stare fixedly at a spot until my eyes dilated. At last unconsciousness! My powers grew marvelously, until I even experienced the sensation of wandering, or being somewhere else."

From the lengthy descriptions of his experiences, it is obvious that he was astral projecting and developing telepathic abilities.

Then, as if the living hell Morrell was experiencing were not enough, his situation took a turn for the worse. A new warden was appointed to direct San Quentin: Morrell describes the warden's initial tour of the solitary cells in *The 25th Man:* "The solitary guard advised the warden, 'Don't take any chances with him. Never trust your face near the door. He would jab your eye out with his finger if he had the chance. That's the man, Morrell, who has the firearms planted somewhere in this prison. He was sentenced to life in here, and he refuses to give up the guns.'

"The warden responded by explaining that he fully intended to find the guns and warned, 'I'm going to put an overcoat on you. It will keep you nice and warm. It might cause you to feel different and maybe tell where the guns are.'"

A new horror had struck San Quentin. The warden, whom Morrell called "The Pirate" because he had only one eye and wore a patch, introduced one of the most abominable torture devices of modern times: the jacket. Morrell was the first to be crushed in its constricting folds, which were designed to squeeze the life out of its victim. When Morrell screamed out in intense pain, the guards responded by gagging him. The first session lasted for four days and 14 hours without pause. For the entire period Morrell was unable to sleep or do anything but experience the unbearable pain.

When the warden finally ordered the jacket removed, Morrell was bleeding and partially paralyzed. He crawled to his water bucket to wash the dried blood from his body, then sank into his straw mattress, where he stayed for a week, unable to rise. The jacket experience brought him to complete despair. "I did not then know that some people are called upon to pay a terrific penalty in order to bring out true understanding of their inherent goodness; that forces of destruction in the form of intense suffering must be brought into play until the old self is annihilated, especially those who come here to perform a mission, perhaps a great service to humanity."

The prison doctor pronounced Morrell dangerously ill and for seven days he had strange visions. At first, he encountered his hatred of his enemies, which eventually dissolved into forgiveness and release. In *The 25th Man*, Morrell described his awakening experience: "A tingling sensation pervaded my frame as I heard a voice, far, far away at first. It rang from the depths of infinite space, but a space bright and luminous. It seemed to speak plainly, almost in my ear. 'You have learned the unreality of pain and hence of fear. You have learned the futility of trying to fight off your enemies with hatred. You have seen that your sword of defense was double-edged, cutting deeply into your own vitals rather than overcoming the evil which has been working against you.'

"The voice continued, 'From today, a new life vista will open up and you will fight from a far superior vantage point. Your weapon will henceforth be the sword of love, and as time progresses and your power unfolds, this new weapon will cut and hew away all evil forces which now oppose you. And to prove the power which envelops your life in this dungeon, even the jacket will have no terrors for you. It will only be a means to greater things. Your life from now on must be a work of preparation, and when the time is ripe for your deliverance, you will know it. The proof will be a power of prophecy to your enemies, not only the day of your ultimate release from this dungeon but also from the prison, when the governor of the state in person shall bring your pardon to San Quentin. Peace and love is yours!"

When "The Pirate" returned he found Morrell calmly smiling at him. The warden shouted, "You must like it, huh?" and again shoved the weakened prisoner back into the jacket. At first, Morrell reexperienced the pain and panic, but it quickly subsided when he induced hypnosis. For three days he astrally traveled, inspecting prisons, jails, and juvenile institutions, and began to form the concepts of a prison reform system. During this time he often found himself in Alameda County somehow attracted to an older man whom he persistently followed and watched. It was the first of many visits to this man.

The jacket device was one of the most effective torture devices ever used in the prison system. It was breaking or killing its victims— all but Morrell. The Pirate was incensed at Morrell's continual smiling response and ordered session after man-killing session. But each time the self-hypnosis allowed Morrell to become master of his body and he astrally experienced events in the outer worlds that he was later able to verify as actually transpiring, including a shipwreck in which he helplessly observed women and children drowning. He experienced numerous past lives and came to understand the karmic patterns set into motion by previous experiences.

"The guns or death!" shrieked The Pirate. "You'll come across with those guns this time or I'll kill you in the jacket."

"I have no guns," Morrell calmly replied, smiling.

"Then to make an extra good job of it, we'll have a double jacketing!" the warden screamed in anger.

The warden was accompanied by the "croaker," a prison physician who judged that Morrell was capable of withstanding more torture, although he speculated that a double jacketing might kill him in five hours. Four days later Morrell was still in the two jackets when a Senate investigation committee came to the prison. Fearing the truth might leak out if Morrell died, they released him from the jacket. To their disbelief he was smiling, although temporarily paralyzed and unable to move. As the warden turned to leave the cell Morrell called out to him, "This is the last time I will ever be tortured in the jacket! One year from today I will get out of this dungeon never to return to it; and better still, four years from the day I leave the dungeon I will walk from the prison a free man with a pardon in my hand."

"He's gone stark mad," laughed the warden as he left the solitary cell.

For months Morrell was left alone and he continued to explore self-hypnosis. While astral projecting, he was often drawn to a "quiet, restful town of fruit and flowers in the interior of California," as he had been many times while wearing the jacket. Here he would be drawn to a school where he was particularly attracted to one of the students, a girl of 12 or 13, who had blue eyes. The faces of most of the students were cloudy, but she appeared very clearly to him.

One year to the day after his own prediction, Morrell waited in anticipation. He had no reason to expect anything, other than the memory of the voice and his own belief. Yet that morning, the new warden of San Quentin walked into the solitary section. To Morrell's amazement, it was the Alameda County man from his astral travels.

"Morrell, I am the new warden," he said. "Three weeks ago, I took charge of San Quentin. From the very first day that I came, I have been busy, investigating your case." He went on to explain that he felt Morrell had never been proven guilty and the previous day he had demanded that the sentence be revoked.

Five years after Ed Morrell entered solitary, the new warden, Major John W. Tompkins, personally led him out of his cell and to the prison hospital, where Morrell spent months recuperating. Several months after he had returned to health, Warden Tompkins appointed Morrell "head trusty" of the prison over the opposition of all prison board officials.

At this time, Tompkins explained to Morrell how he had come to accept the wardenship of San Quentin. Tompkins had been retired when the position was first offered to him, and he had refused it. The new governor of California called him a second time. Tompkins was in his study, absently tapping upon a scratch pad during the telephone conversation. He finally promised the governor that he would think the matter over before giving his decision.

Tompkins hung up the receiver and, glancing at the paper, noticed that something had been written upon it. Seizing the pad, he read the name "Ed Morrell." He looked at it questioningly, wondering about the strange incident. It bothered him, so he called a friend who was a state official. Through the friend, he learned that the name was that of the "dungeon man of San Quentin." The next day he told the governor that he had decided to accept the position.

Four years later, as prophesied, Ed Morrell was handed a pardon by the acting governor, Warren R. Porter. He had been in prison for 15 years. Upon his release, Morrell began to work for prison reform and toured the country, lecturing on the subject. His story caught the attention of Jack London, who decided to fictionalize it for a book, *The Star Rover.* When he found that Morrell did not have the education to write the story, London hired a young journalism student to listen to Morrell's lectures and take notes on all his stories. The student turned out to be the girl in the schoolroom to whom Morrell had often been drawn. She was now an adult and eventually became Mrs. Ed Morrell.

Together, they started their own publishing company and published *The 25th Man,* the true story of Morrell's outlaw and prison experiences. They also founded "The American Crusaders for the Advancement of the New Era Penology," an organization that initiated major prison reform in several states and fostered a national awareness of the need for change.

California governor Warren R. Porter called Morrell "a living example of self-mastery." In the darkness of his dungeon, Morrell discovered his True Self.

In his later years, Ed Morrell lived in Hollywood, California, and was a favorite of motion picture people, who often stopped by to swap stories. He died of pneumonia when I was ten years old, living in the Midwest. So although I have the memories of Ed Morrell locked away within the memory banks of my subconscious mind, he was a parallel life, not a past life.

In summary: A soul is capable of experiencing more than one incarnation at a time and the individual identities communicate with and influence each other on a higher level of mind. My ideas about parallel lives are based not only upon this case history, but also upon hundreds of parallel-life transference sessions I have conducted with other people who were often able to validate their experiences.

But in all fairness, New Age author Ruth Montgomery viewed the story quite differently. She saw me as a "walk-in" of Ed Morrell. She wrote about my case and many others in her book *Threshold to Tomorrow*. To Ruth, the soul originally inhabiting the body of Dick Sutphen willingly stepped out sometime after Morrell died, allowing Morrell's soul to take possession of the body with the original memory banks intact. Morrell could then continue to fulfill his mission, especially with regard to writing and metaphysical communications. According to the information channeled to Ruth through her guides, this is a common practice. Walk-ins are further explained in the next chapter.

Did Ed Morrell have a soul agreement to experience the suffering? It would seem so to me. In his own words, "I did not yet know that some people are called upon to pay a terrific penalty in order to bring out true understanding of their inherent goodness; that forces of destruction in the form of intense suffering must be brought into play until the old self is annihilated, especially those who come here to perform a mission, perhaps a great service to humanity."

Karma is never to punish; it is always to teach.

The prophesied date of Morrell's release from solitary and the governor himself providing his pardon papers four years later both proved true. Obviously, both were destined. The psychic experience of Tompkins writing Morrell's name on the pad, his acceptance of the job as warden, and his investigation of the case were certainly beyond reality. Also the fact that Morrell was drawn to the schoolgirl who later became his wife seems to have been fated.

Strong affinities are usually based upon past experience. My love affair with the American West began when I was a young boy. To this day, I continue to read books and study this period of history. Our home is decorated "cowboy and Indian," with the Winchester on the wall, old photographs, Frederick Remington sculptures, and Mexican-style furniture. Tara and I have always owned horses.

My life is about metaphysics, hypnosis, writing, publishing, and public speaking—the same passions that drove Ed Morrell. It is also interesting to note that shortly after learning hypnosis in the early 1970s, which was well before I knew of Morrell, I made several astral-projection audio hypnosis tapes, which I gave to prisoners in the state prison in Florence, Arizona.

_1 3_

Other Influences

"Our destiny rules over us, even when we are not yet aware of it; it is the future that makes laws for our today."
—Friedrich Wilhelm Nietzsche, German philosopher

As close as I am to the subject of soul agreements and as aware as I am of the factors that influence destiny, I am still surprised when puzzle pieces come together to make a strong point. As an example, Tara and I first visited author Ernest Hemingway's Key West, Florida, home in 1984 while on our honeymoon. His writing room was on the second floor of a carriage house behind the main house, and the room looked out onto a swimming pool. Hemingway wrote with a pencil at a small table while sitting in a leather-slung chair. My visit to that room has always remained with me.

With his short, declarative sentences and terse prose, Ernest Hemingway did more than anyone else to change the style of English fiction in the twentieth century. For his stories and novels, he was awarded the Nobel Prize for literature and the Pulitzer Prize.

While celebrating our 20th wedding anniversary, Tara and I visited the Hemingway home again. My response to his writing room was as intense as the first time, and I read Hemingway and books about him for weeks afterward. *The Hemingway Women—Those Who Loved Him—The Wives and Others,* by Bernice Kert, was a large volume which I verbally condensed for Tara over morning coffee.

In regard to Hemingway's relationship with his mother, Tara said, "She sounds just like your mother." The more of the book I shared, the more intrigued my wife became.

Tara cast Ernest Hemingway's astrological chart. Mother relationships can be read in the aspects of the Moon. "Hemingway had a nine-degree Capricorn Moon. You have a ten-degree Capricorn Moon," Tara said. "His moon was in the Fifth House of creativity, lessons, and emotions. So is yours. No wonder your mothers were alike."

I find such astrological verification comforting. In other words, if your mother had a nine-degree Capricorn Moon in the Fifth House of creativity, lessons, and emotions, your mother made a soul agreement to have a personality just like Hemingway's mother and my mother.

There is an old Zen adage that says, "If you want to know where you are supposed to be, look down at your feet." We chose before birth to be where we are now, doing what we are doing, with the people we are with. We have some degree of free will, and we can change aspects of our lives, but basically, we are living the life we were born to live, in the body we designated for karmic growth.

In previous chapters, we explored past lives, parallel lives, and astrology, but there are other factors that are also soul agreements. If you were born with a natural telepathic sensitivity, this was agreed to while you were still on the Other Side. Being "from elsewhere" and spirit-possession syndrome are also karmic situations—soul agreements I will cover in this chapter.

I will begin with telepathic sensitivity. The following letter from Susan is typical of my daily mail. It represents the kind of problem psychologists, psychiatrists, and counselors, working with standard therapeutic techniques, usually cannot explain or resolve through conventional methods. Susan had attended a seminar retreat and later wrote me about her problem:

Dear Richard,

I am writing to you because I know of nowhere else to turn, and after attending the Lake Arrowhead retreat, I have faith in your advice. Now I wish I had brought it up when we were all together in the mountains, but I was too embarrassed. You see, many years ago I was involved in an on-again, off-again relationship with a man I came to care for very much. Eventually, we went our separate ways, and I haven't heard from him since. After our parting, I did quite well, except for every three or four months when I'd start remembering and be unable to get him out of my thoughts. The feelings would be overwhelming and very distressing.

In time, I stumbled upon a method which helped. When the feelings would begin to overwhelm me, I would put everything down in a letter to him, then seal and address the envelope and put it away. Within a week, the feelings would pass, and I would burn the letter. After five years, it's the only thing that seems to help.

Lately, everything has become more intense. The memories now linger on between the episodes—becoming more disturbing by the month. My life is busy, and I'm concentrating on developing my talents and creating the life I desire. But no matter what I do, the thoughts keep coming back with regularity. I'm desperate to find peace and put it all behind me.

Your books have helped me understand why I'm here, and I know I have to move forward, take risks, and keep my mind open. Is there anything else you can tell me that could explain or help me to resolve this situation?

The following is my response to Susan's letter:

Dear Susan,

Aside from psychological considerations best assessed by a local counselor, there are several psychic considerations. All would result from you being highly empathic (telepathically sensitive), and could manifest as any of six factors: 1) You and your ex-lover may have nearly identical brainwaves. As an example, you may both be alpha-sevens (as could be measured on a brainwave synchronizer) and your shared history has resulted in an ongoing telepathic link. Subconsciously, you are always in communication, but it is only when you have buildup of awareness over several months that it begins to bleed through to your consciousness. Once you relieve the pressure by responding, you open up to begin receiving again. 2) He may be purposely sending telepathic messages to you. 3) He is simply thinking about you, and you are telepathically picking it up. 4) You are occasionally contacting him "out-of-body" on the other side while sleeping at night . . . and the contact lingers. 5) Dreams resulting from unconscious longing are reinforcing the union. 6) He has died and is Earth-bound. Although now in spirit, he lingers near you due to your past relationship. You are picking this up empathically, which generates the effects you are experiencing.

After another letter exchange with Susan, I asked Tara to investigate with automatic writing. She contacted Abenda, who then made contact with a woman in spirit, Eleanor, who knew Susan in the lifetime responsible for the problem. Tara described Eleanor as a petite woman, blonde, dressed in 1800s attire. This is what she had to say:

> Ireland: Susan's name was Franklin. He was a dashing, daring prizefighter within the confines of our prison camp. The guards couldn't break him so they made money from him, by putting him out on the circuit. We remained in the prison camp, and were later shipped to Australia, losing touch with him.
>
> Eventually, Franklin too was sent to Australia, a paralyzed, broken man. He just happened to come to our small camp, men carrying him. I had always looked up to him, and in Australia, I helped care for him many years—as if he were the child I never bore. He loved me in his way, but it was not the love of a woman and man. As his physical condition deteriorated, he called out for others—sisters, past loves, people we did not know.

In this life as Susan, he no longer wishes to fight, but he retains a desperate longing for loving connections that he feels were denied him in that life. As Susan, when the relationship in question ended, she subconsciously used her empathic abilities to retain the connection. Unfulfilled passions karmically carry over as a powerful force. In this case, because she has a natural telepathic ability, she manifested a connection as Dick described in his response. She "feeds" on the connection, then reaches a saturation point and reacts, trapping herself, much as she was trapped in the past life.

Susan should focus her meditations upon vividly visualizing this connection being cut. She can imagine it in many forms: chopping the connection, burning it, dissolving it. It is time for her to find peace, so she can prepare for a new love that awaits.

In Love, Eleanor

When you have experienced an emotional tie with another human being, and you think about them regularly, you are creating a psychic link between the two of you. You do not realize this consciously, but subconsciously you remain in communication. The more telepathic you are, the more likely you will experience the other person's emotions, positive and negative. So if you're feeling depressed and do not know why, it could be that you are perceiving their state of mind. This mental pull could also generate the desire to see each other again. To consciously draw upon someone else in this manner would be using "black power," thus generating negative karma. It is always wrong to manipulate another human being for selfish purposes.

An empathic person will also be influenced by the thoughts and feelings of other people in their environment. To sit on an airplane next to someone who is in the midst of a painful divorce would probably generate feelings of depression in you.

In another case of telepathic sensitivity, a young man named Daniel told me how his life took a downward spiral after he received a raise and moved to a new apartment. "From day one, it seemed like a dark cloud descended upon my life. I moved in over the weekend, excited about living in such a nice place. The complex had a beautiful pool and lots of single girls in residence. But by Monday morning, I awakened depressed. It got worse and worse. On long weekends, with friends up in Big Bear, I'd be fine. But as soon as I got home, I became depressed. I even saw a psychologist. After three visits, she advised I get a thorough physical exam. Nothing. To make a long story short, several months ago I threw a party. A buddy I work with brought a psychic—a woman who does those 900 number phone readings. She had to leave, because the vibes in the apartment were so bad."

"Did the psychic say anything else?" I asked.

"She wanted to know if someone had been murdered there. It scared me. I asked my neighbors about the previous residents. I learned the couple was evicted. Everyone thought he was a drug addict. Neighbors had called the police several times because of their terrible fights. The psychic explained that the vibrations of the previous residents were still there, permeating the walls and appliances. I'm evidently very empathic, and I was drawing in the negativity, thinking it was my own creation."

"Did you move?"

"You bet. And my state of mind returned to normal within a week."

To be telepathically sensitive means a soul agreement was made to be psychic or to be empathic—all different words meaning the same thing. But now I would like to move on to another common unseen influence called "wanderers" and "walk-ins"—different forms of soul agreements.

Since I began researching metaphysics in the 1970s, a high percentage of the people I have worked with have told me that they felt they did not belong here. Something within their psyches was telling them that their true home was elsewhere.

I also had several regressive hypnosis contacts with those I called "Light people" in my early books—people who experienced past lives as nonphysical Light beings. At the time, it seemed to me that they had somehow flunked that advanced level of experience and had been sent back to Earth to experience material reality once again before being allowed to return home.

Today, I'm not sure this was an accurate assumption. Considering other people's investigations, it seems more likely that the Light people incarnated to serve a planet in need of help.

My friend Brad Steiger once wrote a series of "Star People" books. The series was based upon extensive research and seems to generally agree with a study published as *From Elsewhere,* by Scott Mandelker, Ph.D.

According to Mandelker's research (his Ph.D. dissertation), those who feel that the Earth is an alien place usually don't connect their deep sense of being different with the possibility of a non-Earth origin. They are born of Earth parents to fulfill an Earth purpose, and they fall into two categories: "wanderers" and "walk-ins."

Wanderers are souls who have incarnated from a more evolved civilization with memories of their identity and true origin blocked—just as memories of our past lives are usually blocked until investigated using metaphysical techniques. Wanderers volunteered for the purpose of serving humanity. This service may be subtle, or the wanderer may be destined to become a major influence.

Once born, wanderers are as ordinary as everyone else, so it takes a metaphysical effort for them to realize their true identity. According to Mandelker, if they don't make a concerted effort to remember, they can easily become entangled in all the earthly snares everyone else does and never fulfill their plans.

In *From Elsewhere,* the author describes many characteristics of wanderers, including: 1) As children they were thought of as being odd. 2) They are genuinely kind, gentle, peaceful, nonaggressive people. 3) They are not very interested in money or material things. 4) They have a hard time recognizing manipulation and trickery. 5) They cherish great ideals. 6) They have a strong interest in metaphysics and/or UFOs. 7) They have always felt alienated.

On the other hand, walk-ins are souls who participated in a "soul transfer" with a human being who wished to depart from the physical world without dying and without incurring additional karma. The departing soul often feels overpowered and incapable of handling life. An agreement is reached while the person is sleeping and "out of body" on the Other Side. Then the walk-in steps in with the departing soul's memory banks intact. Once the transfer is made, the walk-in doesn't remember what has occurred, but is intuitively driven to clean up the problems of the departing soul. After this task is completed, the walk-in is free to pursue his/her own humanitarian service agenda.

A walk-in's entrance is usually signaled by someone finally getting their life together. The transfer can take place after an accident or near-death experience, but a trauma isn't necessary for the transference to occur. Sometimes, the walk-in appears different to those closest to them. After the old problems are resolved, the walk-in sometimes divorces, drops old friends, or begins a new career.

In the 1980s, Ruth Montgomery was one of the best-selling metaphysical authors in the world, and her books continue to sell well today. When Ruth was writing about walk-ins we occasionally worked together in seminars. For a season, I included a "Hypnotic Walk-in Search" to see if any of the participants were walk-ins. Although everyone wanted to be a walk-in, only one or two people in one hundred perceived being one, and it was a boring session for everyone else. I feel it is important to note that no one "made up" being a walk-in. Statistically, according to Ruth's research, the percentage made sense when compared to the number of souls she said were walking in. In the same seminars, I conducted a "Parallel-Life Transference Session," and almost every participant perceived vivid impressions of being someone else on the planet at this time.

With that information in mind, fast forward to 1996. Tara and I conducted a "Psychic Prophecy Seminar" in Dallas, Houston, Philadelphia, New York City, Riverside, and Los Angeles. The average attendance was one hundred participants per city. In every city, approximately 50 percent of the participants perceived themselves as wanderers. It did not vary, city to city. At a couple of the seminars, no one perceived themselves as a walk-in, while in others we'd find two or three out of one hundred—the same statistics we obtained 14 years before.

The concept of wanderers being here to help may relate to something I shared in my book *Past Lives, Future Loves*. Kingdon Brown is one of the best trance psychics I have ever worked with. Deep in an altered state of consciousness, he shared the following awareness:

There is the impression that this planet was indeed seeded somehow. That the souls here in physical bodies were brought here, and that we are under some incubation, or gestation period that has been going on. The reason this is becoming evident is that there is a life-giving continuity here that does not exist elsewhere in the universe in quite this way. The intelligences are still monitoring our progress. I see . . . I'm now getting this directly. It's like a veil or blinders . . . as the Bible says, "through a glass darkly."

This veil is being removed very carefully to see if we can make this leap, or advancement, without falling backward into disintegration once again as has happened so many times in history. This is what transcendence means. We become something else.

There is an experiment going on with this planet, and the intelligences that are observing it are not taking part directly, for it happens automatically at a certain point. They are observing to see if this time we can accept evolutionary knowledge and true change. There is something here about the relationship of all your past, present, and future physical explorations transpiring in a constant now, and that you will all have to make this change at once. Everybody has to make it. An instantaneous thing, without falling back into a dark age, or a point where all is hidden once again.

Later in this trance-channeling session, Kingdon seemed to expand upon the concept:

Well, I'll have to say this the way it comes to me, but it seems incredible to me. I can't censor it because that would defeat the purpose of this. We are moving toward a point of "etherealization." . . . Ah, we don't really have a word for it in English. We are attempting to move to a place where we do not exist in physical bodies, yet we exist in an ethereal way in which all is totally clear to us . . . as to what has transpired and why we then exist. I'm also receiving with this . . . this is the reason it's so difficult for me to comprehend . . . that at some point when we have reached this degree of evolution, a decision will then be made as to whether or not it will be necessary to continue this planet. It will either be entirely destroyed . . . or something.

What I'm seeing visually is that all of these souls that have been interconnected here and interrelated are fragmenting out the way a dandelion seeds out, and they are going out everywhere. I'm being told that this is why this is an incubating place, where all this care has been placed through centuries of bringing human beings past the state of experimentation into the point of self-creating. But they are self-perpetuating in an ethereal way, or through a spiritual essence, as astral essence.

We create spiritually . . . spiritual propagation . . . ah, there is love. Love is a propagating of the spiritual nature. We will no longer re-create in the way we do now, for we no longer need these bodies, but are in light bodies, and we propagate in a vibration that we call love.

If wanderers come from a more evolved world, maybe a major reason they are here is to help everyone on Earth to evolve to a Light-body level of awareness through the process Kingdon described as etherealization.

Marcia, 34, a pretty blonde with a shy personality, identified with all the aforementioned traits of a wanderer during an altered-state process at one of our retreats. She rarely dated because the men she met were not spiritual. "We have nothing in common," she said. "I've worked at different jobs, but they've never meant much. All I need is enough money to get by. The universe will take care of me."

"Do you have a sense of purpose?" I asked over dinner at our Lake Arrowhead retreat house.

She shook her head.

"I have a feeling that if you become involved in metaphysical service work of some kind, you'll come alive," I said.

Six months later, I received a letter from Marcia: "You were so-o-o-o right. When I got home, I took classes in Reiki energy balancing and began offering my services in the evenings. People I work with were my first clients, and they recommended me to others. With Reiki, I make people feel better, but most important, it gives me an opportunity to share my spiritual beliefs. If my practice continues to grow at the current rate, I'll soon be able to do the work full time. I'm planning to take your Professional Hypnotist Training, so I can also offer past-life regression and accelerate the process."

I've discussed telepathic sensitivity and wanderers/walk-ins as influences that could be affecting your life. Now I'll explore a subject that we touched on in the Diana Mullen and Reverend Fatima Abate chapters—spirit possession syndrome.

Psychologist Edith Fiore, now retired, used to combine psychotherapy with past-life regression to treat spirit possession syndrome (SPS)—problems caused by the spirits of the deceased interfering with the living. Soon after Dr. Fiore began incorporating past-life investigation into her therapy, she recognized that over half her clients exhibited signs of spirit interference. The more she worked with patients suffering from SPS, learning to better recognize the signs and symptoms, the more she became convinced that at some time in their life, nearly everyone is influenced by nonphysical beings to some degree and for varying periods.

Spirit interference ranges from subtle influence, to attachment, to full possession of a living human by a discarnate—the surviving consciousness of a deceased individual. In other words, according to the late William J. Baldwin, Ph.D.—formerly the leading SPS specialist in America—"The entity becomes a parasite in the mind of the host."

"What conditions would allow an entity to attach to you?" is a question I am often asked. My response: Any emotional or physical trauma can open the door to attachment, as can an addiction to drugs, or alcohol, or perhaps even a sexual dependency. After death the earthly desire remains, and in a futile attempt to fulfill its craving, the newly deceased soul clings to living souls who are similarly afflicted.

As an example, a deceased alcoholic might attach to a living alcoholic in an attempt to experience the mind-numbing effects of drink. Long-term anger lowers our vibrational rate, as do extreme fear, jealousy, greed, resentment, remorse, guilt, and the ruthless quest for personal power. Love manifesting as jealousy or an obsessive need to remain with a lover can also keep a soul earthbound.

An ongoing spirit attachment can, in some cases, manifest in lifetime after lifetime, as explained in the opening "Debra Wakefield" chapter of my book *Predestined Love*. To find out why Debra had experienced such an abusive and traumatic life, I regressed her back to the cause. She perceived herself as a female courted by a Roman army officer.

When she refused the man's advances, he cut off the hands of her best female friend, as a warning of what would happen to her if she did not comply with his wishes. The friend blamed Debra for the loss of her hands in the past life and had followed Debra into her current life as an attached entity continuing to blame. Debra had accepted the guilt and was allowing herself, by soul agreement, to be punished over and over again for something that was not her fault. After I removed the entity and I helped Debra to understand the false guilt she had accepted, her life turned completely around.

One of my first contacts with an earthbound entity was in a house I bought situated on an old gold claim in the mountains above Prescott, Arizona. Even my teenage son could perceive the cold, undesirable presence. In time, I set up a session to contact the discarnate—a miner who had worked the area. His partner had hit him in the side with a shovel and he had died slowly, filled with anger. Although he had been dead nearly one hundred years, his side still hurt, and he didn't understand why no one talked to him anymore. Through spirit contact with those who loved him in life, I was able to send him to the Light. After the session, I learned that my new neighbors had occasionally seen manifestations of an old miner in the kitchen as well.

The miner had died slowly, hating his partner. This alone would assure he remained earthbound. Maybe I made a soul agreement to help release him from his entrapment.

Mahatma Gandhi, when shot by an assassin, is said to have verbally forgiven his murderer as he died. He knew not to create a karmic tie or to allow blame, anger, or hatred to keep him earthbound.

In another spirit-possession situation, Kevin was not aware that a nest of entities had attached to him during a period in which he was drinking himself into a nightly stupor. It was only after four weeks in a detox center that he realized that although sober, he was experiencing desires that made no logical sense to him, especially homosexual urges. An understanding therapist explored the entity-attachment potential.

Once Kevin was in an altered state, the therapist drew out a male named Christopher. Through lengthy dialogue, the therapist learned that Christopher was the elected voice of a dozen other souls, all of whom had been alcoholics in life, several of whom had also been gay. This group of parasites was angry at Kevin for denying them their contact high, and when they could not get him to drink, they began mentally prodding him to have sex with a man. The therapist successfully banished the spirits, and today Kevin does not drink and is happily married.

Often an attaching entity can bring accompanying physical pain. Renee was a participant in a group regression session I conducted at the 2003 International Federation of Hypnosis Conference in Long Beach, California. A practicing hypnotherapist, she said that during the back-to-the-cause regression session, she had decided to search out the cause of her ongoing physical pain. "My hip was hurting so badly I could barely sit in my chair," she said.

In the back-to-the-cause regression, I make the suggestion "and in just a moment I'm going to direct you back into your past. You may go back to an earlier time in your present life or you may return to an event that transpired in a previous incarnation. I'm going to count backward from five to one as you move through the time tunnel to your past. On the count of one, vivid impressions will begin to flow into your mind—impressions of a past event that relates to the cause of the karmic situation you seek to better understand."

When the session was over and the participants awakened, Renee explained that in the regression all she saw was a little girl about seven years of age, standing and looking out a window. The girl was terribly sad because her mother had died and her father had no time for her. She had no playmates. "She was so lonely," Renee said. We assumed Renee was seeing herself as a young girl in a past life.

She then asked me if I would individually regress her as a demonstration for the other therapists in attendance. I agreed and proceeded to hypnotize and direct her back to the cause of her physical pain. She again saw the little girl and could not move past the images. In a flash of insight, I realized the little girl was not Renee in the past, but was another entity who was there, right now.

I asked Renee to communicate with the girl. This worked and the girl said her name was Jessica. We discovered she had died at age 10 in terrible pain, which she evidently carried with her into spirit. "I don't hurt when I'm with you," she said to Renee.

Renee, a mother, evidently allowed Jessica to come in, and in so doing, she inadvertently took on the girl's physical pain. Jessica said she did not reside there, but she came and went as she pleased. So this was not a classic case of entity attachment, and I did not know how, when, or why it had happened. Maybe Renee had opened herself to the entity out of empathy.

My next move was to call in the spirit of Jessica's real mother, who asked her daughter to leave with her and go the Light. But Jessica was too fearful to leave Renee's body. Eventually, I had all the other seminar participants come over and lay their hands upon Renee's body. I directed an intense energy buildup, to the point we could feel the heat in the palms of our hands. Then I said, "On the count of three, we'll release the energy into Renee, and, Jessica, this is going to force you out of Renee's body and into your mother's waiting arms. One, two, three!"

It worked. Jessica left with her mother. Renee awakened with a surprised look on her face. She stood up saying, "My hip doesn't hurt. I feel so much better."

Was Renee destined to express compassion to help the child and thus learn a powerful lesson? Was it some kind of karmic payback? I did not know. This is either a random universe and there is no meaning to life, or there is some kind of plan. My life work tells me there is a plan, and the only plan that makes logical sense is karma.

That brings us back to destiny.

A couple weeks after the hypnosis session, I received an e-mail from Renee saying, "I feel okay, but I still have muscle pain. I am starting to think that Jessica might have been there to console me when I felt lonely, as sympathy for my own experiences with loneliness."

As fearful as this form of entity interference is, if Dr. Edith Fiore is correct, most of us have dealt with the influences of nonphysical beings at one time or another in our lives. William J. Baldwin, in his book *Healing Lost Souls,* says, "The term 'spirit-possession' suggests total takeover, which sometimes happens. Entity (an individual being with real and independent existence) or spirit attachment implies connection, clinging, a parasitic invasion of the host by another conscious being. This is a more accurate description of the condition."

How does one avoid such a parasitic invasion? No one can avoid all emotional and physical trauma, so that makes everyone vulnerable. But keeping your vibration rate as high as possible is the best deterrent. Increasing your level of awareness raises your vibrational rate, which is the unconscious quest of everyone on this planet. Although this cannot assure you won't experience SPS, it is difficult for an entity of a lesser vibration to influence an entity of a higher vibration.

Think of the nonphysical spiritual planes as forming a ladder down a well. Each rung of the ladder is a different level, a different vibrational rate. The bottom rungs are damp, dark, cold, and of low vibration. As you climb the ladder, the atmosphere becomes lighter and warmer, and the rate of vibration increases. Your goal is to get to the top and climb out onto the Celestial Plane—the God level. To do so, you must raise your vibrational rate, and this can be achieved more rapidly in the physical body than in spirit.

As with spirit interference, hauntings and apparitions are also caused by earthbound entities. They have the ability to rise above their situation, even on the Other Side, but it often takes hundreds of Earth years for them to realize they are free to go to the Light. In time, they listen to the advice of more advanced souls who are always willing to help. On numerous occasions, while regressing someone into a past life, I have had a subject find themselves on the lower astral plane. The reaction is always the same and is usually described as "confusing, dark, and fearful." The fact that these subjects have been reborn on the Earth plane shows that they have worked their way out of the situation.

At the time of death, you will cross over, leaving the physical body, and again become the spiritual being you actually are. Your vibrational rate at this time will dictate your level on the Other Side. If there are seven astral levels and you have a vibrational rate aligned with the third level, this is as high as you will be able to go. You could not withstand the more intense vibrations on the fourth through seventh levels.

What determines your vibrational rate? Your thoughts, words, and deeds on the Earth plane will determine your level of awareness, which determines your vibrational rate. You were born with a vibrational rate you established in the past. The way you live your life will determine whether you raise or lower the rate during this incarnation. If you changed your way of thinking, speaking, and acting today, your vibrational rate would begin to change tomorrow. Love, positive thoughts, and compassionate actions would raise your level of awareness. Hate, negative thoughts, and trying to control or hurt others either mentally or physically would lower your level of awareness.

Don Weldon, one of my first teachers, said, "It is possible to advance many lifetimes during the time you have left in this life—if you choose to do so."

Nearly 30 years of psychic research have shown me that the line between life and death is not a clear-cut division as is commonly perceived. The dead can influence the living and the living can influence the dead.

When Tara's uncle Vernon Risch was diagnosed with terminal cancer, Tara's mother asked her to work with Vern on a spiritual level. Tara began to mentally project from our home in Malibu to Vern, who was lying in a hospital bed in Anchorage, Alaska. "When he talks to me, it's the same voice I remember so well," Tara would say after awakening from a session. "He tells me he is really scared. I tell him, 'You'll be okay, take my hand.' He doesn't have a spiritual belief system, but I assure him there is nothing to fear, and his mother and grandmother will be waiting to help him when the time arrives."

Vern had been fighting serious health problems for years, but he was a survivor who always managed to amaze everyone by bouncing back to health. However, Tara had informed me a year before that "Vern will die in February 2004."

Sometimes I feel like I live in the "twilight zone." Such statements and unusual manifestations are commonplace in our house. "Really," I will say and nod my head.

Vern died February 1, 2004, leaving behind his wife, Barbara, and five grown children. Tara flew to Anchorage to attend the funeral and support her mother and family during the difficult period.

Three weeks before, the doctors had given Vern three months to live, but a few days before he died, they learned his throat cancer had spread to his lungs. The tumors in his throat were closing off his breathing, and he could no longer verbally communicate.

Tara was talking on the phone with her mother when Vern died. So within the hour, my wife self-induced hypnosis and projected "to the essence of Vern." Moments later she joined her uncle in spirit. "Vern had already looked back upon his body when I arrived," Tara said. "Grandma Gwen and Great-Grandmother Anna were there. Whenever I've seen the grandmas in spirit, they have appeared much younger and more vital than they were when they died. But to meet Vern, they made themselves look older, so he would be more comfortable and accepting of the reunion. The grandmas were all dressed up, which I thought was cute. Two others were with him: a female spirit guide and a man named Frank.

"Vern was really glad to see me. I said to him, 'You realize I'm alive? You've crossed.' He said, 'Yes.' He was still having difficulty talking due to the throat tumors, so I asked that a doctor come and remove the tumors. This happened quickly, and although it was a symbolic releasing, it did the trick. Vern could communicate easily and felt better. Later, Abenda told me, 'Good call on the tumor removal.'

"Grandma Gwen was so excited. She held my hand. She wanted to make a family circle, so we all held hands in a circle. Vern was very quiet, for him. He would ask me little questions, like, 'What do I need to do now?' I said, 'Your spirit guide or Frank will show you; I don't really know what to do. But if you want comfort, go to your mother and grandmother.'

"Vern started following Frank, but Grandma wanted to cook for him. He said, 'I'm not ready to eat.' Frank wanted him to come to his house, but Vern was not comfortable with this. He was afraid he would not remember people's names. He did not remember Frank, so I'm not sure about that association. Vern was worried about his wife, Barbara. I told him, 'She's fine. You've made the transition, and you need to concentrate upon that now.'

"He told me that when he died, it was as if his whole body split in half, and he just lifted out of it. 'I couldn't have stopped it. I was just pulled out and up,' he said."

Tara left for a while to go talk to her own spirit guide. "Abenda told me Vern would connect in and out with me all night while I was sleeping."

When Tara visited Vern's spirit the following day, she experienced a family gathering hosted by Abenda. "Vern, my father, the grandmas, and two grandpas were all gathered around a table with Abenda. I joined them. It was like old times."

To further investigate Vern's death, Tara cast his and Barbara's astrological charts. "Vern was at the most intense aspect on the Midheaven on the hour he died," Tara said. "His wife, Barbara, was also at the most intense aspect in her chart. Vern's death aspects were in play in the House of death. The chart shows he was sick, shows he had cancer, and even the financial drain due to the cancer is indicated. Unusual speech is indicated, which obviously relates to the tumors closing down his throat so he couldn't talk. And his chart shows that people would be there for him at this time. As it was, his wife, all his children and brothers and sisters were there. Loss of a mate is indicated in Barbara's chart. And in my mother's chart, the loss of her best friend. Vern was Mom's best friend."

"So Vern made a soul agreement to die at exactly this time?" I said.

"His death was written on the day he was born," Tara said.

As previously mentioned, when Tara alters consciousness to go up and visit Abenda, her Grandmother Gwendolyn is usually waiting at the bottom of the stairs to hand her flowers. The bottom of Tara's subjective stairway to Abenda is a level just above the fearful lower astral plain. I perceive this as earthbound.

"Grandma is earthbound," Tara says. "She's waiting for her children, her three sons and two daughters, to join her. Vern is the first to cross. Abenda has tried to talk Grandma into moving to a higher vibration, but she doesn't listen. She was deaf in life and she continues to play that role in death. Grandma has manifested a comfortable cottage at this level. She raises flowers, and she still loves to cook. She is always asking me to go with her to the cottage, so she can cook for me. But Abenda does not like me lingering at this level where entity attachment is possible."

As often reported in esoteric writing, thoughts manifest reality on the Other Side in spirit. In her "Cause & Effect" columns, Tara has reported on her continued communications with deceased New Age author Jess Stearn, who was one of her best friends in life. After crossing over, Jess continued to desire food until completing his adjustment to a higher vibration. Jess recently told Tara, "I can think of an earthly place and find myself in a similar place, but it is not the real place, unless I change my structure by going into that reality. The physical body is a heavy mass, compared to how I feel now. But I still feel like I am Jess Stearn, and I will until I take on the role of another name."

I checked turn-of-the-century Theosophical writings on the subject of after-death reactions, and in *The Inner Life—Volume II* by C. W. Leadbeater (1911), I found this:

> [W]e sometimes see the newly dead trying to eat—sitting down to or preparing for themselves wholly imaginary meals, or building for themselves houses. I have actually seen a man in the summer-land building a house for himself stone by stone, and even though he made each of these stones for himself by an effort of his thought, he did not yet grasp the fact that he might just as well have made the whole house for himself, with the same amount of trouble, by a single effort of the same kind. He was gradually led to see that, by the discovery that the stones had no weight, which showed him that his present conditions differed from those which he had been used to on Earth, and so lead him to investigate further.

Thoughts are things, and they directly create a manifestation in spirit. If you loved to go to Lake Louise while living, in death when you think of Lake Louise, you can instantly be there. It won't be the real Lake Louise, but it will be exactly as you remember it.

While on the subject of death, I would like to end this chapter on a more positive note. A famous Zen story tells of a man being chased by a tiger. To avoid being eaten alive, the man leaped off a cliff and grabbed a vine, onto which he hung precariously. As the tiger swiped at him from above, he looked down and saw another tiger far below waiting for him to fall. To make matters worse, a mouse began chewing on the vine. At this moment, the man spotted a luscious wild strawberry growing out of the cliff side. So holding the vine with one hand, he picked the strawberry and ate it. "Delicious."

What happened to the man? Obviously he died a moment later. The Zen point is: The man had a choice of wasting the last moment of his life or appreciating it. He chose to appreciate it.

Should we not live each moment of life as if it were the last moment? That is what you are doing if you manage to live in the ever-present NOW. Every moment is the last moment. There is no other moment than this.

Living in the *now* is a lot easier said than done. But we exist *now* and *now* is all that is. *Now* is outside of time. There is no past in which you were incomplete, and there will never be a future in which you will become complete. Until you accept that you can only exist *now*, you will believe that fulfillment awaits you in an illusory future if you take the proper actions. This belief destroys the experience of *now*, and you continually live in illusion.

This very moment is it. Nothing is hidden. All of your calculating and hoping and planning about how it will be someday . . . all your dreams and plans . . . *this is how it all turned out.* This is all there is. You've been planning all your life for the future, but you will never be aware of the future in the future, you will only be aware of it in the *now*. We do not exist in time. We exist in self.

Use the time component, but never accept it as a reality that entraps you in actions to achieve fulfillment in an illusory future. Always, at this moment, be fulfilled and at peace and in balance.

I am not claiming to have accomplished this level of self-actualization, but I'm working on it. When I catch myself worrying about the future, I tell myself, "Be here now."

1 4

Making the Most of Your Destiny

"We wrestle in our present state with bonds we ourselves have forged—and call it Fate."
—Bhartrihari, Indian philosopher

Although you have destined much of your life with soul agreements, you also have considerable free will. In this chapter, I want to
share some wisdom that can help you to use free will to make the
most of your time on Earth.

"Always follow your heart, it knows the way," reads a hand-
lettered sign on the copyboard beside my computer.

Eastern wisdom says, "Follow the path with a heart."

You could interpret this to mean follow a path that resonates
with who you are, what you want to be, where you find joy, and who
you want to be with.

Or you can look at the wisdom from a higher perspective, which
perceives your spiritual heart to be the center of your soul—your
connection to God. According to the mystics, if you can move your

consciousness from your head to your heart, you will end suffering and attain peace of mind.

The following ideas can help you attain a mind-set to shift consciousness to your heart. When fully applied, the awareness serves as the foundation of an enlightened life.

Let us begin with ego. The more powerful your ego, the more problems you will experience in your life. I define expressions of ego as expressions of fear-based emotions. Your every egoistic thought, word, or action is generated by a fear-based emotion. How could it be otherwise?

A friend said something that irritated you and you responded curtly out of insecurity (a fear-based emotion). You feared your friend did not respect you enough, or you fear your friend thinks she knows better than you, or maybe you fear what she said is true. Or the insecurity has generated an attachment, resulting in anger when your friend didn't live up to your expectations.

Maybe your mate is late, and you want to know why. Your ego demands your lover answer to you. Are you being possessive, jealous, or trying to control?

Your neighbor purchases a new car, causing you to experience envy. Your ego demands an equal level of prestige.

In rising above your fears, you rise above ego and this wisdom erases karma. And the more patient and compassionate you are, the easier it is to evolve beyond ego, resulting in fewer problems in this life and future lives. By being mindful today, you plant the seeds for your own happiness in this life and future lives. The idea is to create all the harmonious karma you possibly can while you have the opportunity.

Gaining karmic merits and avoiding disharmony will result from the choices you make. Life in the physical body is about making growth choices and then experiencing the consequences of your actions through cause and effect. Ideally, you learn through love and wisdom. But if not, there's the old reliable teacher: pain. You touch a hot stove and burn your finger. Touch it again and you burn your finger. Soon, pain teaches you not to touch hot stoves. You can apply this awareness to other aspects of your life.

Love relationships are one of our best ways to grow, because they show us where we are stuck and the fear-based emotions we are clinging to, such as the need to control, judgment, jealousy, possessiveness, and blame.

I will begin by dissecting blame. From a human-potential perspective, blame is self-pity. From a karmic perspective, blame is incompatible with karma and reincarnation. How can you blame someone for playing a part in teaching you the lesson you incarnated to learn? Both parties were acting out their karma.

From a therapist's perspective, psychologist Anne Geraghty in her book *How Loving Relationships Work* says, "The one that apparently initiates a change in the dynamics/agreements of the relationship or lifestyle may not be the one that has really instigated it."

With that in mind, how can you begin to assign blame? When two people are having problems, both are responsible, if only subtly. You might be in therapy for ten years and never uncover the deep churnings beneath the behaviors.

From an astrological perspective, let's say you are a couple and one of you had an affair, which has generated a major crisis in your marriage. A good astrologer will be able to pinpoint a major crisis in both your charts. And if it's in both charts, it was destined to be experienced as a learning opportunity by both people.

When people come to me for past-life regression, more often than not, they are wanting to understand why they are suffering or had to suffer in the past. Why were they sexually molested as a child? Why did their business partner rip them off? Why is their mother-in-law so hateful?

Upon finding the cause, the knowledge often helps people let go of blame. If you see that you hurt the person in another life, it can be easier to justify suffering you agreed to in this life. I always find a multi-life debit and credit system that explains the pain. So all things considered, the next time you find yourself in a conflict with another person, why not accept *all the blame*? After all, you're karmically responsible anyway. And it will end the arguing.

Back to the subject of relationships. Charlotte Joko Beck of the Zen Center in San Diego, California, is one of my favorite teachers. In her book *Everyday Zen* she claims relationships do not work. "There never was a relationship that worked," she says.

Why? Because with any relationship we want something. There are expectations—some subtle, some not so subtle. We try to figure out our relationships—try to find a way to make them work so we can get what we want. The problem is "wanting something" and the resulting expectations.

Beck says: "[W]e often misinterpret what marriage is about. When a relationship isn't working, it means that the partners are preoccupied with 'I': 'What I want is . . .' or 'This isn't right for me.' If there is little wanting, then the relationship is strong and it will function. That's all life is interested in. As a separate ego with your separate desires, you are of no importance to life. And all weak relationships reflect the fact that somebody wants something for himself or herself."

Beck uses a house analogy to make a point about rigidity in marriage and life. There are new designs for beachfront houses that protect the structure from the occasional big storms that flood such residences. In the new designs, when flooded, the middle of the house collapses and the water, instead of destroying the whole house, rushes through the middle and leaves the structure standing.

Flexibly structured relationships function in much the same way, allowing them to absorb shocks and stresses and continue to function. When a relationship is based primarily on "I want" or "I demand," the structure is rigid and will be unable to withstand the pressures of life.

Life will test all relationships like a strong wind beating at the union. If the relationship can't take the beating, then it will have to grow stronger so it can take it, or the couple will be forced to part so that something new has an opportunity to arise from the ashes. From a soul-level perspective, whether the relationship survives isn't as important as the karmic lessons learned by the two individuals.

Relationships offer abundant gifts in the form of opportunities to learn, although the lessons may not feel like a gift during times of testing. But that is what we're here to experience. We incarnated to learn about the futility of expectations and to rise above all the fear-based emotions, including those fears that cause us to want to control those closest to us. Even your ideals are expectations in disguise. When you're attached to the way you think someone else should be, you'll be unable to appreciate life as it is.

In his book *Take Your Time: Finding Balance in a Hurried World*, Eknath Easwaran says, "Most relationships begin to fall apart through disagreements, and disagreements are not settled by argumentation and logic. They are resolved—or, more accurately, dissolved—through patience. Without patience you start retaliating, and the other person gets more upset and retaliates, too. Instead of retaliating with a curt reply, slow down and refrain from answering immediately. As soon as you can manage it, try a smile and a sympathetic word. So much of the richness of life is to be found in companionship that I cannot stress strongly enough how important it is to heal bonds that have weakened and to bring freshness back to relationships that have grown stale."

Adding a little paradox to this mix, it seems to me that the less you try to force things, the faster they seem to happen. The more you try to force things, the longer you usually wait for results.

"Don't push the river," say the mystics and some therapists. The more enlightened you become, the less you will be concerned with outcomes. This advice is usually accompanied by admonitions to live in the present—the eternal *now*. You can't change the past and the future is yet to unfold. If you can "be here now" you will reduce your level of anxiety.

When you live with expectations and desires, it follows that you naturally want to control outcomes. You want things to unfold in your favor. But you can't control outcomes in life. The best you can hope to do is increase the odds through wisdom.

If you are desiring a particular outcome, step back and ask yourself, "What is the fear associated with the outcome?"

Explore the fear, including the worst that might happen if things did not turn out in your favor. If you're committed to an outcome, the fear will be related to loss: the loss of love, of control, finances, or self-esteem. Which applies to your situation?

Then ask yourself, "What if I could take the fear out of my desire?"

If there were no fear, the outcome would not matter. Logical.

So we're back to resolving fear, a subject I write about a lot, because I'm working on it all the time.

As New Agers, we believe we can create our own reality, and I know this to be true when it comes to finding happiness, fulfillment, and an abundant life. Reality is created by the way we view and accept what is. But don't confuse this with controlling outcomes that affect other people.

In other words, if you want that special man to fall in love with you, that is not within your power to control, no matter how many hypnosis mind-programming CDs you use. The same is true with winning the pageant, getting your book accepted by a major publisher, or desiring a beautiful sunset.

Expectations and the desire to control do not work. Both are fear-based emotions, which we incarnated to rise above.

Many New Agers believe in controlling their thoughts. But it cannot be done. You can catch yourself when you are thinking negatively. You can use thought-stopping techniques that condition you, over time, to reduce fearful thinking. But out-and-out control of your thoughts is not an option. Life in the physical body is about making growth choices and then experiencing the consequences of your actions through cause and effect. What you can control is your own behavior—your own actions.

Back to the subject of love: Loving your mate or lover unconditionally can make you free. But for most of us, love becomes attachment. Conditional love is attachment. Attachment is a bondage. And if love is bondage, it is also an illusion.

According to Osho in *Love, Freedom, Aloneness: The Koan of Relationships,* we say we want to be free. Freedom is the goal, but if we are totally free we're alone. So we must be brave enough to be alone if we want to experience freedom.

But we're not brave enough to be alone. We want someone else in our life. We fear loneliness. We fear being unoccupied. We started out looking for love, but maybe we were really looking for attachment. Our need may have been attachment all along. Love was the way to attain it—the bait.

A love of unconditional acceptance will not become attachment. But the moment you say to your partner, "Love only me," you begin to possess him or her. And in possessing, you're making your lover into an object—a thing—something to be used.

According to philosopher Immanuel Kant, to treat another person as a means to an end is an immoral act. In other words, if you see your lover as being there for your gratification, or to fulfill your sexual desires, or to provide something else for you, you are reducing your partner to an object. Thus you are in bondage to each other.

But once you are in bondage, you will desire freedom again. Whatever you get, you will become bored with, and whatever you desire but do not get, you will long for.

Maybe you want to be free while still possessing your partner, causing a struggle.

Osho says, "I want to be a free person, and still I want you to be possessed by me; you want to retain your freedom and still possess me—this is the struggle. If I possess you, I will be possessed by you. If I do not want to be possessed by you, I should not possess you. Possession should not come in between. We must remain individuals and we must move as independent, free consciousness. We can come together, we can merge into each other, but no one possesses. Then there is no bondage and then there is no attachment."

The idea is to establish love without possessiveness, without jealousy or clinging. There should be no judgment, no blame, no expectations, and no attempts to control. The soul can grow only in freedom—unconditional love provides freedom.

To carry this idea a little further, let us explore the subject of security.

"Live Dangerously" read a sign on Friedrich Nietzsche's wall.

Nietzsche was a German philosopher who taught that traditional values represented a "slave morality." His quest for personal liberation is associated with some New Age thinking today. He maintained that all human behavior is motivated by the will to power—the power over oneself that was necessary for creativity. As role models for what Nietzsche called an "superman"—a liberated human being—he mentioned Socrates, Jesus, Leonardo da Vinci, Michelangelo, and Shakespeare.

When questioned about the Live Dangerously sign, Nietzsche claimed it was to remind him that "My fear is great."

Nietzsche advocated "letting go" and living life as a great adventure.

What about you? Your inner nature calls for you to quest and learn and grow.

"No," you say. "I want security. Aliveness is dangerous. I cannot follow my inner nature."

But when you try to protect yourself from change to maintain security, more often than not you will experience a reduction in your life force. Your soul will suffer.

Living dangerously means when you are offered a choice, you take the growth choice—not the safe choice, the comfortable choice, or the socially acceptable choice. You choose based upon what generates aliveness for you.

Deep within, you know what is best for you. And it will always be to strive for more awareness. Never allow yourself to reach a level of self-satisfaction where there is no new challenge. For most of us there will be no new growth without the agitation of discontent. So the idea is to carefully study your dissatisfactions, for they will tell you what you are about to leave behind and possibly point to a new future direction.

"Only to the extent that we expose ourselves over and over again to annihilation can that which is indestructible arise within us. In this lies the dignity of daring. We must have the courage to face life, to encounter all that is most perilous in the world," said philosopher and psychotherapist Karlfried Graf Durkheim.

Challenge generates aliveness, which makes life worth living.

In his book *Callings* Gregg LeVoy says, "The desire to protect ourselves from change probably does more harm to the flowing of human life and spirit than almost any other choice, but it is imperative to understand something about security: It isn't secure! Everything about security is contrary to the central fact of existence: Life changes. By trying to shelter ourselves from change, we isolate ourselves from living. By avoiding risk we may feel safe and secure—or at least experience a tolerable parody thereof—but we don't avoid the harangues of our consciences. It's almost axiomatic that the important risks we don't take now become the regrets we have later. In fact, I was once told that if I'm not failing regularly, I'm living so far below my potential that I'm failing anyway."

"Courage is the willingness to be afraid and to act anyway," says Stewart Emery, author and creator of the Actualizations trainings.

Your life will always mirror what you put out. Fearful thoughts and actions will generate a fearful life of *no* action. When you hold back, your life holds back. But when you are willing to be afraid and act anyway, committing yourself to life, you generate aliveness and open up to the full potential of joy.

All change and growth involve three steps:

• Discontent: Because of outside conditions or your own inner feelings, you decide your current situation no longer works for you.

• Turmoil: Normally, a period of mental turmoil follows in which you challenge your old beliefs. You begin to fantasize how things could be different. This transitional period could last a day or years—until something happens.

• Action: Something or someone helps you to make a decision, or an opportunity presents itself, or you manage to attain clarity. Once this happens, you take action and, ideally, manifest a more satisfying life.

But out of fear we resist change, cling to the status quo, and do everything in our power to keep people and things in their familiar static positions. If you're in a good relationship, you certainly don't want your union to spin off in some unexpected direction that will cause you anxiety. You want things to remain just as they are, solid and predictable. But soon suffering arises, because life is constantly changing.

< It is your resistance to what is that causes your suffering. Life is change. Change is what is. If not today, then tomorrow, next month, or next year. Everything in your life will eventually change. >

Trouble starts with our desire for permanency. Desire is a matter of living in the future—of sacrificing the present for the future. And desires always disappoint. If you don't get what you desire you become frustrated. If you do get what you desire you'll still be frustrated, because what you desired will never live up to your expectations. Sooner or later you'll find you were chasing illusions.

And permanency is a great big faulty assumption, because it simply does not exist. >

But what if you could lock up life so that permanency were possible? Nothing would ever change. Tomorrow would be a repetition of today. Next year, everything the same. Five years down the road, exactly the same. Boring! Static! Depressing! It is the *not knowing* that makes life exciting and generates aliveness.

So the idea is to be courageous enough to embrace change, knowing that your soul is in search of new experiences to provide growth. Growth is why you incarnated upon the Earth in the first place. But you can't experience growth living a static life. A static life may protect you from some problems, but at what cost and for how long? Stagnation is a process of drying up—allowing your life to become dull, colorless, lifeless. No aliveness. No joy. Watch some TV, go to work, come home, watch some TV, go to work, come home. Treadmill.

Even if your actions in a quest for growth cause you pain, at least when you're hurting you know you're alive. And the pain will generate more action, which will lead to more aliveness. Soon you'll find yourself back among the living.

If your life has become lifeless, what can you possibly fear from change? Explore your dissatisfaction, allow time for confusion, and then make up your mind and act to manifest a more satisfying life.

Pema Chödrön says in her book *Comfortable with Uncertainty:* "A warrior accepts that we can never know what will happen to us next. We can try to control the uncontrollable by looking for security and predictability, always hoping to be comfortable and safe. But the truth is that we can never avoid uncertainty. This not-knowing is part of the adventure. It's also what makes us afraid."

Pema continues, "If we find ourselves in doubt that we're up to being a warrior-in-training, we can contemplate this question: 'Do I prefer to grow up and relate to life directly, or do I choose to live and die in fear?'"

I hope you will choose to grow up and relate to life directly. As I said in the beginning of this chapter, the goal is to move your consciousness from your head to your heart. When these ideas are fully applied—when fully lived—the awareness will help you to make the most of your destiny. You have the power and the ability to end suffering and attain peace of mind—which is the foundation of an enlightened life.

1 5

A Final Look at Soul Agreements

< We make soul agreements to help us learn the lessons we most need to learn for our soul growth. We all predestine our lives to different degrees, depending upon the challenges we decide to accept this time around. In this final chapter, I will share three short case histories that will summarize some of the concepts shared in the final chapters.

In his last life as a male living in Nova Scotia, Wayne attempted to control his wife to the point she rebelled and left him. A soul pattern of needing to control others had destroyed relationships in several incarnations, so prior to entering this life, he made a soul agreement to be born with astrological configurations assuring an accepting personality. On a soul level he hoped to learn to maintain a relationship by accepting his mate as she is. But Marianne, his wife in this life by soul agreement, is a woman he tried to control in a past life, so she is especially sensitive to any form of manipulation. In their current relationship, Wayne is quietly withdrawing from his wife.

"Withdrawal is another way to try to control," I said. "Let Marianne be who she is. If you don't, you're going to make the same mistakes again."

"But I don't confront her about the things that upset me," Wayne said.

"Yes, you do. By withdrawing you're expressing your displeasure in a passive-aggressive way, Through your actions, you're trying to force her to be who you want her to be."

As part of my hypnotic explorations with Wayne, I directed him to explore two of his parallel lives. In addition to being the 42-year-old male working as a software engineer in Los Angeles, he has a female parallel self in her mid-fifties living in Sydney, Australia. She has worked with electronics and computers all her adult life, so has probably inspired Wayne in his career work. A second parallel self is a male teenager in Hong Kong, and we did not yet find any perceptible influences. The parallel lives are soul agreements on the part of all three people.

After directing Wayne to move up into Higher Self and connect with his spirit guide, I asked him about being a walk-in or a wanderer. He was neither. But when I questioned him at this level about entity attachment, he explained that during his college days he smoked a lot of grass. "I was definitely influenced by earthbound entities during that stoned period of my life," he said.

"Was this by soul agreement?" I asked.

"Not exactly," Wayne said. "I had free will, but on a soul level I knew if I self-medicated, as I had with alcohol in past lives, earthbound entities would drag me further down. Thankfully, Marianne stepped in and helped me rise above my drug problem."

The next hypnosis session tends to explain some different kinds of soul agreements:

Sophia, 43, has a telepathic sensitivity that has served her in some ways and complicated her life in others. She does not see herself as psychic, but calls herself "a good guesser." In her work as a saleswoman in a high-fashion store in Beverly Hills, California, her sixth sense comes into play when helping hard-to-please women.

"Sophia always knows what I'll like and what flatters me," said one of her customers.

On the other hand, when Sophia spends time with anyone who is having a problem, she deeply perceives the other person's suffering and becomes depressed herself.

While Sophia was in deep hypnosis in Higher Self, I asked her about being born with psychic ability. "It was a choice I made in spirit," she said. "Because I had developed this ability through practice in an Irish incarnation, I was allowed to invoke it again as one of my carry-overs."

"What is a carry-over?" I asked.

"A previously developed ability that you carry over into your next incarnation," she said. "I also carried over artistic ability, an affinity for mathematics, plus well-developed hand-eye coordination."

"This is by soul agreement?"

"Yes. Of course. But there are negative carry-over agreements as well."

"Can you explain?"

"All my life I've been plagued with headaches. This relates to a Middle Ages incarnation in which I was a member of a group that hung a man. Later, we found out he was probably innocent and I experienced horrible guilt. In every incarnation, I carry over headaches as a soul reminder of what I did."

"Self-punishment?"

"I have not yet suffered enough to resolve the guilt," she said.

"Is there anything else you can share?"

"I was born with a predisposition to asthma. I was a male soldier in the Civil War. I smoked a pipe from age 14 until I was nearly 80. Health-destroying indulgence in one life can carry forward into a future life."

The next case history explores a sexual soul agreement:

Daniel and his wife, Carol, are in their late thirties and have an open marriage. Early in their dating life, they discussed how their previous mates had affairs, they had affairs, and so had most of their friends. The affairs usually destroyed the relationships. They decided monogamy did not work and agreed to make it all right to enjoy "sport" sex with other people. After nine years of marriage, they remain happy and committed to each other. Most of their outside sexual involvements are shared experiences, but both are free to enjoy other people on their own as well.

According to Tara, their astrological composite spells this out loud and clear. "These two would never have a traditional marriage," she said upon examining their chart.

"So not only is their union by soul agreement, their sexual relationship was also predestined?"

"Absolutely," Tara said.

As part of a joint hypnosis session with Daniel and Carol, I suggested a chakra-link experiment. I would hypnotize Daniel and regress him back into a past life that would help to explain their sexual orientation today, if such a lifetime existed. Carol would also be hypnotized and observe what Daniel was experiencing in the past life. They agreed to the exploration and as part of the induction, I had them both visualize their top three chakras as being connected.

In past-life regression, Daniel told of a South Seas island lifetime. Sex was not an issue with the islanders. Everyone enjoyed open relationships and the resulting children lived with their mothers. No questions were asked about paternity.

When I awakened Daniel, he smiled, stretched, and said, "Carol was there, too."

"I know I was," she said. "I was the one who gave you the necklace, wasn't I?"

Daniel nodded, smiling from ear to ear.

In separate follow-up Higher Self sessions, I learned that both Daniel and Carol are wanderers. Maybe they originally crossed over from a more evolved world to help humans rise above what Daniel and Carol call "the repressive sexual mores instilled by organized religion."

Because I write about karma, Dharma, and soul agreements, people often ask me if I know exactly how much of my life is destined? No. Like most people, I only seem to question fate when things are not going my way. But when challenges arise, I do not roll over and give up, saying, "Oh, it's destined to be, so why fight it?"

Wisdom erases karma, so in response to challenges, I work to learn the needed lesson in hopes of avoiding a negative outcome. My philosophy—the ideas shared in this book—mitigates the emotional impact of problems. However, during trying times, I often turn to Patrick Smith, a close friend and my favorite psychic, and to

Lee Holloway, my personal astrologer, who keeps me alerted as to personal ups and downs as well as business timing. Last year, she told me not to work with the public over four specific weeks. So I did not book any seminars or appearances during that time and stayed home to work on my writing. This was not blind trust, but a decision based upon 12 years of experiencing Lee's astrological accuracy. Experience is a powerful teacher.

≪ Some mystics call the world a "teaching device." In other words, your soul agreements put you in this place, at this time, with these people, living in an unstable world, to give you an opportunity to learn. How you respond to your tests will dictate whether or not you pass the class. ≫

If you want an "A" in Earth-life class, the best response is to learn to be in the world but not *of* it—to be a witness of life without being caught up in the drama.

This is easier said than done when confronted with personal problems, terrorist threats, and war. Physical escape might be a consideration if there were somewhere to go. But your personal problems will follow you anywhere. Terrorists even strike in remote South Sea islands. Nuclear fallout is global.

The mind is your only refuge—to go within the calm center of the cyclone. Whenever you are upset, stressed, or suffering, your expectations are in conflict with what is. You think things could or should be different than they are.

≺ The way you view life can create a cyclone. ≻

Or the way you view life can keep you in the calm center of the cyclone.

Endnotes

1. I assume the blocks Abenda mentions are built into an individual's astrological configurations. In plotting a chart, Tara will sometimes tell me an individual has a block to establishing a one-to-one relationship, or a block to monetary security. These are karmic situations to assure a particular lesson is learned this time around. The term "intensity factors" means anything from the intensity of a personality, to the intensity of a relationship, to the intensity in which life lessons present themselves. Elders and Masters are highly evolved, enlightened souls who assist us in our learning. When the student is ready the teacher will appear—unseen help from spirit during your waking hours and direct teaching while you are deep asleep. "Vibrational port" relates to an avenue through which we leave the other side on our journey to attach our soul to the Earth plane once again.

2. Upon reading her astrological chart, Katherine said, "In a past-life regression directed by someone else, I experienced a lifetime where my husband took me out of the closet basically only for sexual pleasure. I was from a privileged family, but that didn't help my plight."

3. According to some Eastern thinking, knowledge fills your mind and feeds your ego. The goal is to be innocent, to function from a state of not-knowing. When you feel that you know nothing, you feel wonder and awe. To stand in awe and wonder is to be ready for God.

4. Patti quickly regained her ability to throw off the diseases after a day or so of purging her body.

5. Father John is one of the spiritual mentors Fatima channels.

6. Some of the material in chapter 12 was originally published in *Past Lives, Future Loves* by Dick Sutphen (Simon & Schuster Pocket Books 1978) and as an epilogue by Dick Sutphen in *The Star Rover* by Jack London (Valley of the Sun Publishing 1987).

Bibliography

Bach, Richard. 1977. *Illusions.* New York: Delacorte Press.

Baldwin, William J. 2003. *Healing Lost Souls: Releasing Unwanted Spirits from Your Energy Body.* Charlottesville, VA: Hampton Roads Publishing Company.

Beck, Charlotte Joko. 1989. *Everyday Zen: Love & Work.* San Francisco: Harper & Row.

Chödrön, Pema. 2002. *Comfortable with Uncertainty: 108 Teachings.* Boston: Shambhala.

Drosnin, Michael. 1997. *The Bible Code.* New York: Simon & Schuster.

———. 2002. *Bible Code II: The Countdown.* New York: Viking/Penguin Group.

Easwaran, Eknath. 1997. *Take Your Time: Finding Balance in a Hurried World.* New York: Hyperion.

Frissell, Bob. 1994. *Nothing in This Book Is True, but That's Exactly How Things Are.* Berkeley, CA: Frog, Ltd. Books.

Geraghty, Anne. 2003. *How Loving Relationships Work: Understanding Love's Living Force.* London, England: Vega.

Leadbeater, C. W. 1911. *The Inner Life*. Wheaton, IL: The Theosophical Publishing House.

LeVoy, Greg. 1997. *Callings: Living the Authentic Life*. New York: Harmony Books.

London, Jack. 1987. *The Star Rover*. New epilogue by Dick Sutphen. Malibu, CA: Valley of the Sun Publishing.

Mandelker, Scott. 1995. *From Elsewhere*. New York: Birch Lane Press Books, by Carol Publishing Group.

Osho. 2001. *Love, Freedom, Aloneness: The Koan of Relationships*. New York: St. Martin's Griffin.

Rajneesh, Bhagwan Shree. 1984. *The Book: An Introduction to the Teachings of Bhagwan Shree Rajneesh*. Rajneeshpuram, OR: The Rajneesh Foundation.

Schnell, Donald. 2000. *The Initiation*. Makawao, Maui, HI: Inner Ocean Publishing.

Stearn, Jess. 1984. *Soulmates*. New York: Bantam Books.

Sutphen, Dick. 2000. *Mind Travel*. Niles, IL: Nightingale Conant.

———. 2001. *Self Mastery*. Niles, IL: Nightingale Conant.

———. 2002. *Hypnology*. Niles, IL: Nightingale Conant.

Contacts

The individuals listed below are open to contact. The information is accurate at press time:

Reverend Fatima Abate, *healer, Brazil and Los Angeles, CA. www.messengers-of-light.org or phone: 310-822-6770.*

Judi Chase, *e-mail: Judi@Earthharmonyfoundation.org.*

Dan Cleary, *hypnosis instructor, pain relief specialist, Ft. Lauderdale, FL. www.danclearyhypnosis.com.*

Patti Conklin, *medical intuitive and healer, Hartwell, GA. www.patticonklin.com.*

Meghan Hansen, *record producer, Los Angeles, CA. www.purpledolphinmusic.com.*

Shauna Hoffman, *therapist and "whodunit" producer, Santa Clarita, CA. www.whodunitcruises.com.*

Lee Holloway, *astrologer, Los Angeles, CA. e-mail: LeeHollowayCA@aol.com.*

Don Schnell, *Swami, Sedona, AZ. www.spritualjava.com,*
    e-mail: Donald@spiritualjava.com.

Patrick Smith, *psychic, Malibu, CA, and Dallas, TX.*
    e-mail: theirishseer@msn.com.

Dick and Tara Sutphen, *Box 38, Malibu, CA 90265.*
    www.dicksutphen.com
    e-mail Dick: sutphenseminars@hotmail.com
    e-mail Tara: tarasutphen@yahoo.com

About the Authors

Dick Sutphen is called "America's foremost psychic researcher" by Simon & Schuster Pocket Books, and "America's leading past-life therapist" by the Mind Body Spirit Festivals in London, England, and Sydney, Australia. In addition to writing the million-copy best-seller *You Were Born Again to Be Together*, he has authored 19 additional metaphysical books—seven for Pocket Books—and three multi-CD albums for Nightingale Conant.

Dick is primarily known for his books and seminars on reincarnation and mind programming. Through his Valley of the Sun Publishing, he created the first hypnosis tapes in 1976. Today there are more than 300 Sutphen self-help and metaphysical CDs in worldwide release.

Since 1976, more than 175,000 people have attended a Sutphen seminar, retreat, or expo workshop. Dick and his wife, Tara, appear regularly at the Mind Body Spirit Festivals in London, England, and Sydney, Australia, and at dozens of New Age expos and festivals in the United States. He's often a featured speaker at professional hypnotist conventions.

The Sutphens live with their children, dogs, cats, and horses in Malibu, California. For more information, write Dick at Box 38, Malibu, CA 90265 or visit www.dicksutphen.com.

Tara Sutphen is the author of *Blame It on Your Past Lives* and three series of audio CDs, which include guided meditations and mind programming. She has written many articles about the psychic sciences for national women's magazines such as *American Woman* and *Women's Own*. Tara is a talented psychic and specialist in the psychic sciences, including automatic writing, palmistry, and esoteric astrology.

Tara's meditation CDs are among the most popular in the Valley of the Sun line. "Destiny of Peace," a video meditation, was her personal response to the Iraq War. She recently interviewed Native American shamans in Montana and Utah for a forthcoming video to be titled "Whispers on the Wind."

Tara has often used automatic writing to assist her husband in his research, as is evidenced in Dick's books *Earthly Purpose* (Pocket Books) and *With Your Spirit Guide's Help* (Valley of the Sun). Her "Cause & Effect" column is a regular feature in *Soaring Spirit* magazine and on the couple's website.

HAMPTON ROADS
PUBLISHING COMPANY, INC.

Thank you for reading *Soul Agreements*. Hampton Roads is proud to publish an extensive array of books on the topics discussed in *Soul Agreements*, topics such as accessing past lives, astrology and divination, personal relationships, and more. Visit us on the web: www.hrpub.com.

Northumberland Dreaming
A Past Life Remembered
Mary Rhees Mercker

High drama from an exciting era in English history, this is the past-life biography of a Crusader knight who fought under Richard Lionheart in the Holy Land, and later witnessed the signing of the Magna Carta.

Paperback • 424 pages
ISBN 1-57174-086-4 • $14.95

Under the Inquisition
Linda Tarazi, Ph.D.
Foreword by Jess Stearn

When a therapy patient undergoes regression therapy, her detailed description of life in Spain during the Inquisition becomes one of the most vivid and historically accurate past-life accounts on record.

Paperback • 680 pages
1-57174-058-9 • $14.95

Dear Companion
The Inner Life of Martha Jefferson
Kelly Joyce Neff

Relive the early days of American life as Neff recalls her past life as Thomas Jefferson's wife Martha; complete with her recollections of their days at their Virginia home, Monticello.

Paperback • 632 pages
ISBN 1-57174-075 • $14.95

The Red Snake trilogy
By George McMullen

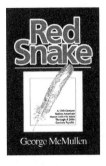

Red Snake

Red Snake is a seventeenth-century Huron Indian with whom psychic McMullen converses. Walk with him as he hunts, fights his tribe's enemies, and courts his wife. This is a fascinating portrait of a now-vanished culture before the coming of the Europeans.

Paperback • 160 pages
ISBN 1-878901-58-3 • $9.95

Running Bear
Grandson of Red Snake

McMullen's trilogy continues with a still thriving Native American culture. As we watch through Running Bear's eyes, however, the Europeans are largely supplanting that culture, starting a cycle of devastation we're still feeling the effects of today.

Paperback • 168 pages
ISBN 1-57174-037-6 • $10.95

Two Faces
Walking in Two Worlds

Two Faces, a half-breed, is raised by his Huron family before going out into the white man's world of the early 1700s. Combining a native's feel for the land with a white man's mentality, Two Faces adapts to his new world and forges a life for himself.

Paperback • 232 pages
ISBN 1-57174-071-6 • $11.95

Born Many Times
George McMullen

Psychic McMullen brings the spirit of a Native American shaman to life, weaving a fascinating tale of his journey through a multitude of lives. Share in his journey through Atlantis to Ancient Egypt and beyond.

Paperback • 224 pages
ISBN 1-57174-131-3 • $12.95

Return of the Revolutionaries
*The Case for Reincarnation
and Soul Groups Reunited*
Walter Semkiw, M.D.

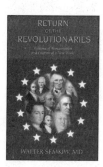

Presenting evidence that facial structure, personalities, and peer groups stay the same lifetime after lifetime, Semkiw shows how America's revolutionary heroes are reemerging today as the force behind America's spiritual rebirth. Semkiw even includes hundreds of startling photos and clues to tracking your own past lives.

Paperback • 464 pages
ISBN 1-57174-342-1 • $16.95

Tantra of Sound
How to Enhance Intimacy with Sound
Jonathan Goldman and Andi Goldman

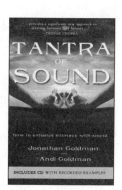

Celebrated musician Jonathan Goldman teams with his wife, Andi, a holistic psychotherapist, to create an innovative approach to developing self-awareness. The result is a first-of-its-kind book that introduces the healing power of sound to the realm of intimate relationships and personal growth.

Paperback with Bonus Audio CD • 208 pages
ISBN 1-57174-432-0 • $15.95

Naked Relationships
Sharing Your Authentic Self to
Find the Partner of Your Dreams
Jan Denise

A newspaper columnist dispensing self-help and relationship advice gives you the keys to ending the cycle of bad relationships by focusing on the most important relationship of all: your love and full acceptance of yourself.

Paperback • 160 pages
ISBN 1-57174-306-5 • $12.95

Tune into Love
Attract Romance through the
Power of Vibrational Matching
Margaret McCraw
Foreword by Alan Cohen

Using Vibrational Matching in her counseling practice, McCraw helps singles and couples find and maintain the relationship they desire. You will learn how to attract the partner of your dreams, and how to keep that relationship strong, loving, and vital.

Paperback • 256 pages
ISBN 1-57174-430-4 • $14.95

Linda Goodman's Star Cards
A Divination Set Inspired by the Astrological and
Numerological Teachings of Linda Goodman
Compiled and written by Crystal Bush
Illustrated by Frank Riccio

Compiled by Goodman's trusted friend and former business partner, this beautiful set represents a completely new divination system that stays true to the Goodman ethic of making cosmic concepts easy for anyone to grasp and use for daily guidance. Consult the cards anytime for answers to your most pressing questions on love, work, and life.

Set includes: 33 full-color cards, 96-page hardcover book
ISBN 1-57174-185-2 • $24.95

Hampton Roads Publishing Company

. . . for the evolving human spirit

HAMPTON ROADS PUBLISHING COMPANY publishes books on a variety of subjects, including metaphysics, spirituality, health, visionary fiction, and other related topics.

For a copy of our latest trade catalog, call toll-free, 800-766-8009, or send your name and address to:

HAMPTON ROADS PUBLISHING COMPANY, INC.
1125 STONEY RIDGE ROAD • CHARLOTTESVILLE, VA 22902
e-mail: hrpc@hrpub.com • www.hrpub.com